Learning the
HP-UX
Operating System

Hewlett-Packard Professional Books

Learning the HP-UX Operating System

Marty Poniatowski

For book and bookstore information

http://www.prenhall.com

Prentice Hall PTR
Upper Saddle River, New Jersey 07458

Library of Congress Cataloging-in-Publication Data
Poniatowski, Marty

    Learning the HP-UX Operating System / Marty Poniatowski.
      p. cm. -- (Hewlett-Packard professional books)
    Includes index.
    ISBN 0-13-258534-0
    1. Operating systems (Computers) 2. HP-UX. I. Title. II. Series
QA76.76.063P65   1996
005.4'3--dc20   96-18464
                                            CIP

Editorial/production supervision: *Joanne Anzalone*
Manufacturing manager: *Alexis R. Heydt*
Acquisitions editor: *Karen Gettman*
Editorial assistant: *Barbara Alfieri*
Cover design: *Talar Agasyan*
Cover design director: *Jerry Votta*
Manager, Hewlett-Packard Press: *Pat Pekary*

 Published by PTR Prentice Hall
Prentice-Hall, Inc.
A Simon & Schuster Company
Upper Saddle River, New Jersey 07458

The publisher offers discounts on this book when ordered in bulk quantities.

For more information, contact:
Corporate Sales Department
Prentice Hall PTR
1 Lake Street
Upper Saddle River, NJ 07458

Phone: 800-382-3419, Fax: 201-236-7141
E-mail: corpsales@prenhall.com

Printed in the United States of America
10 9 8 7 6 5 4 3 2 1

ISBN 0-13-258534-0

Prentice-Hall International (UK) Limited, *London*
Prentice-Hall of Australia Pty. Limited, *Sydney*
Prentice-Hall Canada Inc., *Toronto*
Prentice-Hall Hispanoamericana, S.A., *Mexico*
Prentice-Hall of India Private Limited, *New Delhi*
Prentice-Hall of Japan, Inc., *Tokyo*
Simon & Schuster Asia Pte. Ltd., *Singapore*
Editora Prentice-Hall do Brasil, Ltda., *Rio de Janeiro*

PREFACE

Welcome to <u>Learning The HP-UX Operating System</u>. I have worked with hundreds of HP-UX customers over the years, and written over fifty technical articles two books on HP-UX. In all of these endeavors my focus has always been taking the complex and making it easier to understand so users can be productive quickly. These are my main priorities in <u>Learning The HP-UX Operating System</u> - make HP-UX easy to understand and get you started quickly.

Is HP-UX complex? In many respects it is. I'll tell you which aspects you can ignore, and which aspects you just have to bite the bullet and deal with. I'll also do my very best to make the complex aspects you have to deal with a little easier to understand, both through example and by providing just enough background.

HP-UX is an operating system based on UNIX. There was a time when UNIX-based systems were intended to be used by only scientists on their "private" computers. Now HP-UX is found as much in commercial environments as it is in scientific and engineering groups. This would not have been possible with the original UNIX operating system I worked with many years ago. It is because of the many advancements in UNIX-based operating systems, most importantly HP-UX, that it can now be considered for commercial applications.

The good news for you as a potential user of HP-UX is that many of the advancements that have taken place are in the area of the user interface and ease of use. To have been an early UNIX user, I can assure you from first-hand experience, would have been a more difficult experience.

Now HP-UX is really on a roll. If you have seen an HP-UX system recently, you have seen not only the commercial functionality that has become an important part of HP-UX but also the user interface and multi-media advancements. But does this mean that HP-UX is easier to use? Does this mean you'll have to issue fewer of those scary UNIX commands such as **grep** and **awk**? Are all of those slick backgrounds, colors, and graphics just a mask over what is still an operating system developed for a bunch of PhDs? You will have to answer these questions yourself after you have read and worked with this book. I hope you'll go through this whole book in which I'll give you both background and how to information on becoming an HP-UX user.

You probably already have some experience with a computer operating system with which you enjoy working. I hope this book shows you that HP-UX is also an enjoyable operating system to use. I have worked with several proprietary operating systems that I also thought were great. Working with UNIX is certainly more of a challenge, however, I have seen hundreds of users come over from proprietary operating systems to HP-UX quickly and enjoy the experience along the way.

I also want you to know you can trust me. I have worked with so many new HP-UX users that I know what you need to know. I won't waste a lot of time with System V this and Berkeley that. I'll give you what you need to know and provide only relevant background. I'll fast forward past the history lesson of UNIX and jump into the state-of-the-art UNIX implementation in HP-UX.

This article series is written in such a way that you don't need experience with any particular operating system to read it. Whether your experience is with a mainframe operating system, VMS, MPE, DOS, MS Windows™, or any other operating system, it won't matter when it comes to understanding what I provide. Experience with any operating system will be enough to easily follow along with the topics I cover in this book.

<u>Learning The HP-UX Operating System</u> is comprised of the following chapters:

- Chapter 1 - <u>HP-UX Components and Typical Installations</u>

- Chapter 2 - <u>Login and Password</u>

- Chapter 3 - <u>The HP-UX File System</u>

- Chapter 4 - <u>Permissions, the **ls** Command, and File Name Expansion and Wild Cards</u>

- Chapter 5 - <u>File System Related Commands</u>

- Chapter 6 - <u>HP-UX Tools</u>

- Chapter 7 - <u>HP-UX Networking</u>

- Chapter 8 - <u>Shell Programming</u>

- Chapter 9 - <u>HP Visual User Environment</u>

- Chapter 10 - <u>The vi Editor</u>

- Chapter 11 - <u>HP-UX System Administration Introduction</u>

- Chapter 12 - <u>Programming with SoftBench</u>

- Chapter 13 - <u>Command Summary</u>

Conventions Used in the Book

I don't use a lot of complex notations in this book. Here are a few simple conventions I've used to make the examples clear and the text easy to follow:

$ and #   The HP-UX command prompt. Every command issued in the book is preceded by one of these prompts.

italics   Italics is used primarily when referring to a menu pick or other such selection.

bold and " "   Bold text is the information you would type, such as the command you issue after a prompt or the information you type when running a script. Sometimes information you would type is also referred to in the text explaining it and the typed information may appear in quotes.

<----   When selections have to be made, this indicates the one chosen for the purposes of the example.

Acknowledgments

Like my other books, there were too many people involved in helping me with this book to list them all. I have decided to formally thank those who wrote sections of the book and those who took time to review it. I'm still not sure if it takes more time to write something or review something that has been written to ensure it is correct. Aside from the reviewers and those who wrote sections of the book I must thank my manager, John Perwinc. Not only did John put up with my writing this book but he also *encouraged* me to write both this book and my previous books. He also sponsored the training I required to gain the knowledge to write this book and supported me in every way possible.

A group that requires special thanks is my family who put up with a workstation on our kitchen table for the year I was writing this book and for putting up with the many late nights I spent at customer sites and HP offices working on the book.

Debbie Lienhart

Debbie manages the SoftBench Framework and User Interface team of Hewlett Packard in Fort Collins, CO. She has been a software engineer and manager at Hewlett Packard in Fort Collins for thirteen years. Before joining the SoftBench team, Debbie worked on EE CAD systems and debuggers. In a previous life she was a technical illustrator for a geologic engineering consulting company. She has a BA in Geography from Humboldt State University and an MS in Computer Science from Colorado State University. Debbie wrote the "Programming With SoftBench" chapter of this book.

Gerry Fish

Gerry was an instructor with Hewlett Packard Customer Education Services for over eight years. As an instructor he wrote and taught many HP-UX and UNIX programming, administration, and client/server implementation courses. He has written numerous shell scripts for HP customers as well as shell scripts to manage over thirty systems in the HP Boston Education Center. Gerry wrote the Shell Programming chapter of this and my other books.

Gerry is currently working with the Hewlett Packard Medical Products Group (MPG) where he is an Information Technology Consultant working on a new client/server architecture for MPG's internal business applications.

Reviewers

I'm not sure what makes someone agree to review a book. You don't get the glory of a contributing author but it is just as much work. The primary reviewer of this book is Karen Kilgore of Hewlett Packard in Mountain View, CA. I greatly appreciate her hard work in ensuring the correctness of this book.

Marty Poniatowski

Marty has been a Technical Consultant with Hewlett Packard for ten years in the New York area. He has worked with hundreds of HP-UX customers in many industries, including on-line services, financial, and manufacturing. He has worked extensively with both HP server and workstation installations.

Marty has published over fifty articles in computer industry trade publications. In addition to this book, he is the author of <u>HP-UX 10.x System Administration</u> (Prentice Hall, 1995) and <u>The HP-UX System Administra-</u>

tor's "How To" Book (Prentice Hall, 1993). He holds an M.S. in Information Systems from Polytechnic University (Brooklyn, NY), an M.S. in Management Engineering from the University of Bridgeport (Bridgeport, CT), and a B.S. in Electrical Engineering from Roger Williams University (Bristol, RI).

Chapter 1

HP-UX Components and Typical Installations

HP-UX Components

HP-UX is an operating system. Your hardware is controlled by HP-UX. When you save a file to your tape drive, read the manuals stored on CD-ROM, or move your mouse, it is HP-UX that controls the hardware. Every stroke of your keyboard requires HP-UX to interact with your hardware.

The operating system also controls how system resources are distributed. HP-UX is both multiuser and multitasking. You can have a small number of users, or as many as thousands of users, if you have an HP-UX corporate business server, who need to use system resources in order to get their job done. This can result in many processes that need to be executed simultaneously in order for people to get their jobs done. HP-UX manages what processes will get what system resources at what time and for what time interval.

As a new HP-UX user, you may not care very much how HP-UX handles hardware and ensures many users get the resources they need. There is, however, a great deal of interaction you may have with HP-UX in order to get your job done. This interaction includes managing your

1

user files and directories, printing files, and handling electronic mail messages.

Here are some characteristics of HP-UX you will want to know about as you learn HP-UX in this book:

> **User Environments Are Bundled With HP-UX** - The HP Visual User Environment (HP VUE) and Common Desktop Environment (CDE) are bundled with HP-UX systems. These user environments provide advanced features that help you organize your working environment to make you more productive. I'll cover HP VUE in an upcoming chapter. They can also be used to reduce the amount of interaction you have with the operating system. You can, for instance, use icons to manipulate files and directories. You should, however, still know the HP-UX commands to perform these tasks. I'll cover manipulating files in one of the upcoming chapters even if you decide to use icons.

> **Networking Is Bundled With HP-UX** - Your system administrator probably has networking enabled on your HP-UX system already. I'll talk more about networking when I cover some typical installations.

> **HP-UX is Multitasking** - HP-UX can perform many tasks at the same time. This means a lot can be going on at the same time, all of which must be coordinated by HP-UX.

> **HP-UX is Multiuser** - Bring on the users. The very high end HP-UX systems can handle thousands of simultaneous users. Most of the burden of managing users falls on the shoulders of your system administrator. There may, however, be

times when you care about the number of users logged into a system or which specific users are currently logged in. I'll cover some commands related to users.

Keep in mind these characteristics as you develop an understanding of HP-UX. Many of these may prove to be important to you.

Typical HP-UX Installations

There is no such thing as a typical HP-UX installation. There is such a thing as a typical Personal Computer installation. It consists of a processor, keyboard, mouse, display, windowing software, and applications. Sure, there are all kinds of other options you can include, such as CD-ROM, network connections, and so on. But most Personal Computers have the features I described.

There is also a typical mainframe installation. This would be a huge, expensive computer to which many terminals are connected, running business applications. Here, too, there are many options, but a mainframe typically consists of a lot of terminals connected to one big system.

Again, is no typical HP-UX installation. HP-UX is an "open" system and can, therefore, be set-up in a varity of different ways. One of the big advantages of open systems is flexibility. One of the particularly big advantages of the HP-UX product line is that it is highly scalable. This means you may end up with one or more larger systems that are shared among users or a highly distributed environment in which each person has their own workstation.

Let's take a look at some simplified HP-UX installations.

Highly Distributed

Figure 1-1 shows a highly distributed HP-UX environment. You're in fat city if this is the type of environment you have, because each user has their own workstation or X station on which to work. If you have your own workstation then in all likelihood how you go about consuming your system resources is up to you. The number of users on a workstation (remember multiuser?) is typically one - and that is you. All the tasks being managed on a system are being managed for you (remember multiuser?). This means your fate is in your own hands. I will cover the basics of system administration in an upcoming chapter, in the event you are working in a highly distributed environment and want to perform a few checks on your system and perform some lite system administration.

Let's talk about the X stations shown as a potential device on this network, because an X station is a specialized device. Everyone I work with in the HP installed base has at least a couple of X Stations, some as many as several thousand, because of the unique void they fill. An X Station is similar to a workstation in that it has the same graphics display, keyboard, mouse, network connection, and user interface. The difference is that an X Station has an "X Processing Unit" instead of a system processing unit. What this means is that programs run on a workstation someplace on the network, but all of the X processing is done locally on the X Station. This is great if you wish to manage fewer workstations, because an X Station requires virtually no system management.

X Stations and workstations are similar in many respects. From a user perspective there is no difference between an X Station and workstation in a properly configured environment. Because there are many options when running X Windows, it is sometimes difficult to determine what might be the best solution in a specific computing environment. In some cases, two solutions may address an objective equally effectively.

The first bit of business to take care of is the basic terminology. An X Station does not run an application such as your 3D design tool or database, your host does this. Because the X Station controls the window in which your application is displayed, it is the X server. The host on which your application runs that accepts commands from the X server is the X client. This terminology sometimes takes a little getting used to. Thinking of the host running an application as an X client and the place it is being displayed as the X server is somewhat the reverse of what you might first think, but keep in mind that the X server is controlling the X window.

Note that there is also a server system on this network. This may be a file server on which the workstations on the network store their files. This makes backup and file management in general much easier for the system administrator. It is also possible to use the server as a compute server. You may have some very compute-intensive tasks that would bring your workstation to its knees and should therefore be run on a more powerful system. You can take this process one step further and use software that runs on all the systems on the network, and that can determine which system is in the best position to run your job, and dispatch your job to that system.

HP Task Broker is just such a tool for distributing computational tasks. With HP Task Broker you can do the following:

- Distribute computational tasks among not only HP-UX workstations but other UNIX workstations as well.

- "Load Balance" a group of UNIX systems by transparently finding the most available server for a computational task.

- Form a "computational cluster" that can distribute computing among several systems much less expensively than mainframe or super computer.

- Receive the results on your computer regardless of where computing has taken place on the network.

• Set-up the Task Broker systems on the LAN
by updating the central Task Broker file on one
system.

The highly distributed environment also takes advantage of the bun-
dled networking and user environments that come with HP-UX. The networking allows systems to communicate on an on-going basis and
provide such functionality as allowing your files to be stored anywhere
on the network, such as on the server, and have this be completely transparent to you. Most all HP-UX workstation users and X station users run
HP VUE or CDE on their systems. Since the user interface is also bun-
dled, there is little or no configuration for a system administrator to perform to enable these.

I will cover many networking commands in a later chapter that you
may be interested in. These commands allow you to perform such tasks
as logging in to remote systems and performing work, copying files to
remote systems, and so on.

The systems in a highly distributed environment tend to run somewhat more independently and are more dedicated to a local user than a
centralized environment.

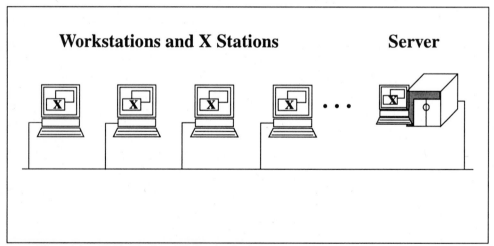

Figure 1-1   - Highly Distributed Workstation Environment

Although I plan on covering HP VUE in an upcoming chapter, it is hard to talk about a highly distributed environment without talking about HP VUE and some of its features and ancillary components. Figure 1-2 is an HP VUE screen shot.

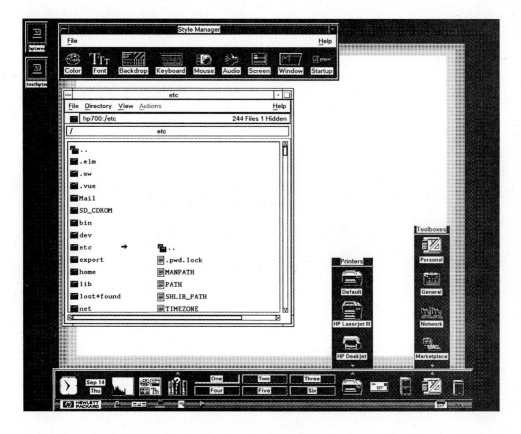

Figure 1-2 HP VUE Screen

Although I will cover HP VUE in detail in an upcoming chapter, I'll describe a few of the features of HP VUE to give you an idea of how powerful a user environment this is with the following list:

• Login Manager - Allows you to start a work
session by logging in through a graphical
screen. I will include several Login Manager
examples in Chapter 2.

• File Manager - The File Manager provides a
graphical means of navigating through your
local HP-UX filesystem as well as remote file
systems. Files and directories can be moved,
copied, deleted, and added. These functions are
performed by selecting an icon and then selecting the desired function from the menu.

• Workspace Manager - A workspace is an
organization of the user environment comprised
of windows and icons. Six workspaces are
shown in the screen shot. You can switch
between these six workspaces by just clicking
the mouse on the workspace to which you wish
to switch.

• Style Manager - You can customize most
every aspect of your user environment with the
Style Manager, such as colors, fonts, backdrop,
keyboard, mouse, audio, and so on.

• Session Manager - Allows you to save your
customization so you can restore to the same
state when you next login.

• Icon Editor - Create your own icons, including text and audio.

You can also take this user interface one step further with HP's multimedia product MPower. Among the functions you can perform with MPower are:

Sharing Information - With MPower's SharedX and whiteboard you can simultaneously view information on several systems.

Messages With Meaning - You can send electronic mail messages with MPower that include audio, graphics, and video. This means that if you are working on a document that includes graphics, you can send a mail message to a co-worker that includes the graphics as well as an audio message that you record.

In addition to all that you can do with HP-UX, it is a fact of life in the computing world that you need personal computer applications to do your job as well. There are a variety of solutions to help you in this area. Here are a list of some of the more popular solutions:

HP 500 - This is a dedicated pentium-based server that runs PC applications and displays them in X Windows to your workstations and X stations.

HP Wabi - HP Wabi runs several Microsoft Windows applications on your HP workstation or X station. Microsoft Windows API calls are translated into X Windows calls.

Insignia® SoftWindows™ - The Intel instruction set is emulated by SoftWindows so all PC software runs on your HP workstation or X station.

Macintosh Emulation Software™ (MAE) - Why stop at Microsoft Windows? Mac users are people, too. MAE runs popular Mac applications and provides a Mac look and feel to your HP workstation or X station.

Highly Centralized

Because HP-UX systems are highly scalable, you can have one small system dedicated to one user, as described in "Highly Distributed," or you can have a single system dedicated to thousands of users! These users are connected to the centralized system with Personal Computers they may already have, with X stations, or with terminals. This type of environment is shown in figure 1-3. Over the past few years I have seen most highly centralized installations going from almost all terminal connections to almost all Personal Computer or X station connections. Who wants to work on a dumb terminal if they can have a Personal Computer running a windowing environment or an X station running HP VUE or CDE?

The centralized system takes a lot of care and feeding by the system administrator. With many users logged in and many processes per user

and per application, there is a lot to track. Such a highly centralized system may have many Central Processing Units, several GigaBytes of
main memory and TeraBytes of disk storage. If you are connected to
such a system you can rest assured that it is carefully monitored to
ensure you're getting the best possible performance.

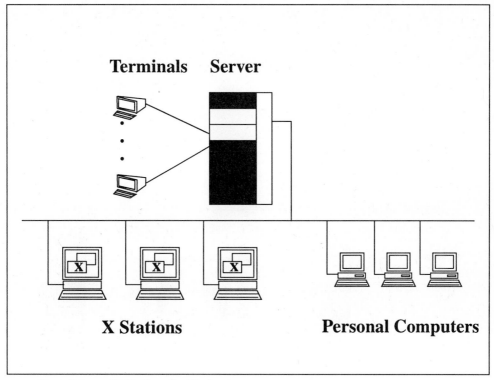

Figure 1-3   Highly Centralized Environment

Multiple Servers (But You Don't Know It)

Why stop at one centralized server? There is advanced HP-UX functionality that allows several centralized systems to work together. This
means you login to any one of several systems and go about your work.

This environment is shown in Figure 1-4. You may later login to a different system and go about your work in exactly the same manner. There is a substantial amount of work that goes on in the background by your system administrator to achieve this level of functionality, but who cares? As long as it is transparent to you and your application runs great, it really doesn't matter.

In this environment you are also connected to the servers with a Personal Computer, X station, or terminal. The end result from your standpoint should be nearly identical to the "Highly Centralized" solution.

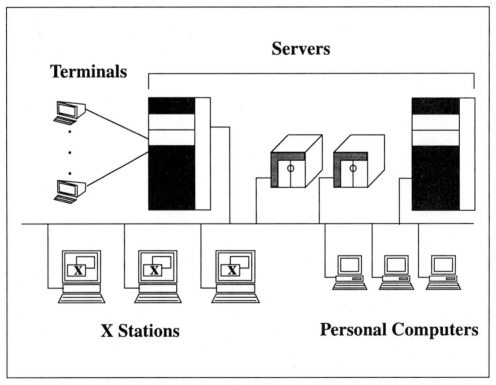

Figure 1-4   Multiple Servers Environment

In the next chapter I'll cover Login and Password. This will include background information on the file that contains information about users on the system (**/etc/passwd**) and the file that contains background information about how users are grouped together (**/etc/group**). I'll then cover some sample login sessions so you'll be in a good position to get started logging in to your system.

Chapter 2

Login and Password

Upper and Lower Case

HP-UX cares a lot about upper case and lower case. This is true for login and password as well as topics we will cover in upcoming sections such as file names. For now it is sufficient for you to know that you must type your user name exactly as it has been assigned to you. If it is all in lower case, then you'll have to type it in lower case to be given access to the system. The same is true of your password; that is, you must type it exactly the same as it was originally defined. Don't type **Denise** if your HP-UX system thinks your name is **denise**. HP-UX systems are stubborn this way. Once the system is told to look for a **denise**, it will not recognize a **Denise**. These could actually be defined as two different users.

Before we get into some sample logins, it might be helpful to you to see how the system keeps track of you as a user and the group to which you belong.

The /etc/passwd File

This is one of those times when I think it would be helpful to share with you some information about system administration. The **/etc/passwd** file contains information pertaining to users. We commonly refer to this as the password file. If you have a highly centralized environment, then all users are attempting to connect to the same system, so all users access the same **/etc/passwd** file. If you have multiple servers or a highly distributed environment, your system administrator may have setup some advanced networking functionality that allows systems to share only one copy of the **/etc/passwd** file over several systems. Regardless of how the password file is managed, its contents may prove revealing and interesting to you. The following is an entry in the **/etc/passwd** file:

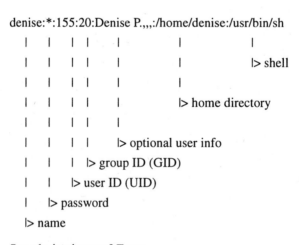

```
denise:*:155:20:Denise P.,,,:/home/denise:/usr/bin/sh
  |   |   |  |    |          |            |
  |   |   |  |    |          |            |> shell
  |   |   |  |    |          |
  |   |   |  |    |          |> home directory
  |   |   |  |    |
  |   |   |  |    |> optional user info
  |   |   |  |> group ID (GID)
  |   |   |> user ID (UID)
  |   |> password
  |> name
```

Sample **/etc/passwd** Entry

This may at first seem like more information than the system needs to know about you. The optional information in this file can include any information the system administrator wishes to keep about you. Here is a description of each of these fields:

name. The user name assigned to you. This name should be easy for you to remember. When sending electronic mail or copying files from one user to another, the easier it is to remember the user name the better. If you have a user name on another system and it is an easy name for others to remember, you may want to assign the same user name on your HP-UX system. Some systems don't permit nice, easy user names, so you may want to break the tie with the old system and start using sensible, easy to remember user names on your HP-UX system. Remember, there is no security tied to the user name; security is handled through the user's password and the file permissions.

password. This is your password in encrypted form. If an asterisk appears in this field the account can't be used. If it is empty, you have no password assigned and can log in by typing only the user name. I strongly recommend that you have a password which you change periodically. Every system has different security needs, but at a minimum every user on every system should have a password. Some features of a good password are:

• A minimum of six characters that should include special characters such as slash, dot, asterisk, and so on.

• No words should be used for a password.

• Don't make the password personal such as name, address, favorite sports team, etc.

• Don't use something easy to type such as 123456, or qwerty.

• Some people say misspelled words are acceptable, but I don't recommend using them. Spell check programs that match misspelled words to correctly spelled words can be used to guess at words that might be misspelled for a password.

• A password generator that produces unintelligible passwords works the best.

• Make sure no one knows your password but you. Someone causing damage to the system using your login could be difficult to explain.

user ID (UID).   Your identification number. Every user on your system should have a unique UID. There are no conventions for UIDs. Typically, use UIDs less than 100 for system-level users.

group ID (GID).   The identification number of the group. The members of the group, and their GID, are in the **/etc/group** file. The system administrator can change the GID assigned if you don't like it, but you may also have to change the GID of many files. As you create files, your UID is assigned to the file as well as the GID. This means if your GID changes some time after users of the same group have created numerous files and directories, you may have to change the GID of all these. I usually save GIDs less than 10 for system groups.

optional user info.   In this space the system administrator can make entries, such as the user's phone number or full name. You can leave this blank, but if your system administrator manages many systems or networks with many users they may want to add the user's full name and extension so if they need to get in touch with the user, the information is there.

home directory.   The home directory defines the default location for all of your files and directories. This is the present working directory at the time of login.

shell.   This is the startup program you will run at the time of login. The shell is really a command interpreter for all of the commands the user issues from the command line. I recommend using the default POSIX shell (**/usr/bin/sh**), but there are also three traditional popular shells in the HP-UX environment: C shell (**/usr/bin/csh**); Bourne shell (**/usr/old/bin/sh**); and Korn shell (**/usr/bin/ksh**). We'll talk more about shells in general in upcoming chapters.

You Are Grouped With Others

Since you are part of a group as defined in the **/etc/passwd** file, I thought it might be worthwhile to show you what this file looks like. Groups are often overlooked in the HP-UX environment until the system administrator finds that all his or her users are in the very same group, even though from an organizational standpoint they are in different groups.

The **/etc/group** file contains the group name, encrypted password, group ID, and list of users in the group. Here is an example of an **/etc/ group** file:

```
root::0:root
other::1:root, hpdb
bin::2:root,bin
sys::3:root,uucp
adm::4:root,adm
daemon::5:root,daemon
mail::6:root
lp::7:root,lp
tty::10:
nuucp::11:nuucp
military::25:jhunt,tdolan,vdallesandro
commercial::30:ccascone,jperwinc,devers
nogroup:*:-2:
```

This **/etc/group** file shows two different groups of users. Although all users run the same application, a desktop publishing tool, some work on documents of "commercial" products, while others work on only "military" documents. It made sense for the system administrator to create two groups, one for commercial document preparation and the other for military document preparation. All members of a group know what documents are current and respect one another's work and its importance. The system administrator will have few problems among group members who know what each other are doing and will find these members don't delete files that shouldn't be deleted. If the system administrator puts all users into one group, however, it may be that more time is spent restoring files because users in this broader group don't find files that are owned by other members of their group to be important. Users can change group with the **newgrp** command.

We'll come back and talk about how the group you are in relates to the permissions that you and others have on files. But now let's move ahead to the actual login process.

Some Sample Logins on a Terminal

When you attempt to login to the system using a terminal (we'll get to some graphics examples soon) you'll see a screen that looks something like the following:

```
Welcome to New York System

HP-UX Release 10.x


Login:
```

What appears on the screen for you to login is controlled by the system administrator. He or she edits the **/etc/issue** file that contains the information to be printed on your terminal.

The prompt that appears is requesting your user name. Since you are now well aware that you have been defined a user name and password, you can proceed with the login process by entering this user name:

```
Welcome to New York System

HP-UX Release 10.x


Login: denise
Password:
```

When you type your user name and hit the *Enter* (sometimes called *Return*) key, you will see you user name appear after the login prompt. When you type your password, however, you will not see this appear for security reasons.

If you type in your user name and/or password incorrectly, you will get the same error message, which reads *Login incorrect.* This is because the system does not want to reveal to someone who is attempting to break in to your system whether the user name, password, or both are incorrect. If the system were to report that the password was incorrect then the hacker would know that he or she had used a valid user name. The less that is revealed under these circumstances the better. If you type your user name incorrectly and this is the name of a user who does not exist on the system at all, you will still be asked for a password.

If you make a mistake while typing your user name or password the "backspace" key will not typically work. You can hunt for the key that represents a backspace on your system, or you can just type in the wrong information and then type in the correct information on your next attempt. Keep in mind, however, that you are permitted a specific number of attempts to log in by your system administrator.

After you have successfully logged in, you will again see what your system administrator has set up. There may be a message of the day or simply a prompt that allows you to begin working. By default a lot of Copyright information is displayed for you to read, but this may have been removed by your system administrator so as not to clutter your screen.

Some Sample Logins Using HP VUE

If you are running HP VUE or CDE you have a whole different login environment to look forward to. Figure 2-1 shows the HP VUE login screen with the *Options* box selected.

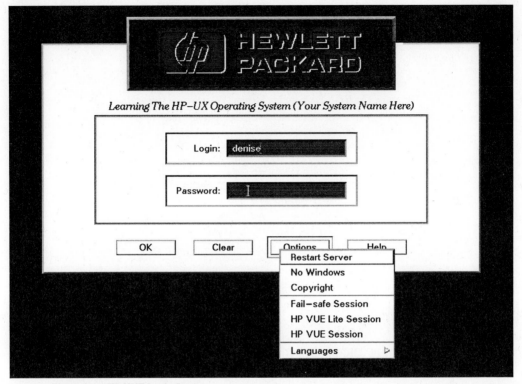

Figure 2-1   HP VUE Login Screen

You can see that among the many options you have is to select the language you wish to use, or come up using no windows and go through the procedure for logging into a terminal as described in the previous section.

In this case denise has typed both her user name and password, without the password displayed, and is about to log in. The *Backspace* key works in HP VUE so if you make a mistake here you can use it.

If, however, you do make an error and type in either a wrong user name or password, you will see something similar to Figure 2-2:

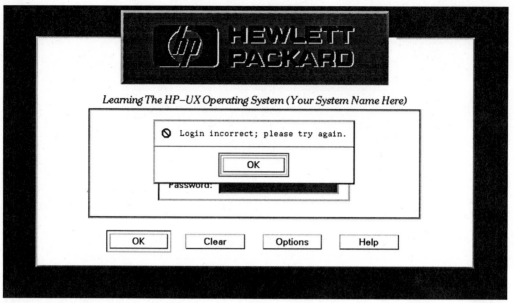

Figure 2-2   Login Incorrect Message

The "Login Incorrect" message will not appear until both a user name and password have been entered. After a successful login to HP VUE you will see an environment similar to that shown in Figure 2-3. This same figure appeared in Chapter 1and in that chapter I described some of the components of HP VUE.

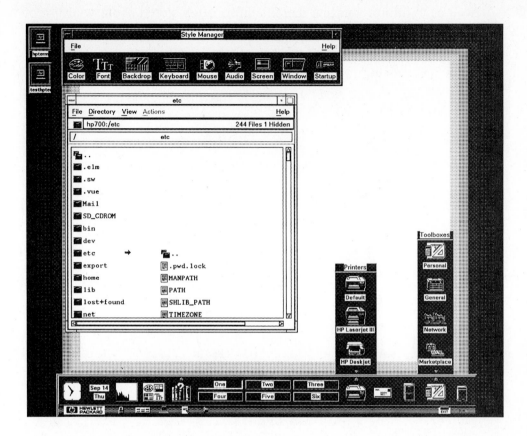

Figure 2-3 HP VUE Screen

Your system administrator has information about both your successful and unsuccessful login attempts. The two commands your system administrator can issue are the **last** command to view successful logins and logouts and the **lastb** command to view bad login information. Information about logins and logouts is kept in the file **/var/adm/wtmp** and information about unsuccessful login attempts is kept in **/var/adm/btmp**. Although you are not in a position to run these commands as a new user, I want to make you aware that these commands exist. You should know that information is kept specifically about login attempts as well as to inform you that there is information stored about your use of the system that can be viewed by your system administrator.

Here is an example of what your system administrator would see if he or she were to run the **last** command:

```
# last -40

castro      network     Tue Oct 3 15:03 still logged in
preston     network     Tue Oct 3 14:58 still logged in
smith       ftp         Tue Oct 3 14:56 still logged in
cooper      ttyp1       Tue Oct 3 14:55 still logged in
simms       network     Tue Oct 3 14:53 still logged in
bileski     network     Tue Oct 3 14:51 still logged in
moore       ftp         Tue Oct 3 14:50 still logged in
winder      network     Tue Oct 3 14:49 still logged in
hunter      network     Tue Oct 3 14:48 still logged in
sacko       network     Tue Oct 3 14:47 still logged in
blinn       network     Tue Oct 3 13:46 - 13:56  (00:10)
kerry       ftp         Tue Oct 3 13:45 - 13:56  (00:11)
keller      network     Tue Oct 3 13:43 - 13:55  (00:12)
barry       ttyp2       Tue Oct 3 13:43 - 13:53  (00:10)
rampart     network     Tue Oct 3 13:41 - 13:59  (00:18)
albert      ftp         Tue Oct 3 13:41 - 13:52  (00:11)
domontel    network     Tue Oct 3 13:40 - 13:56  (00:16)
preston     network     Tue Oct 3 13:39 - 13:59  (00:20)
cooper      network     Tue Oct 3 13:37 - 13:59  (00:22)
moore       ttyp4       Tue Oct 3 13:36 - 13:55  (00:19)
bileski     ttyp5       Tue Oct 3 13:35 - 13:58  (00:23)
hunter      ftp         Tue Oct 3 13:33 - 13:56  (00:23)
sacko       ftp         Tue Oct 3 13:30 - 13:48  (00:18)
marlo       network     Tue Oct 3 13:26 - 13:56  (00:30)
everoni     ttyp8       Tue Oct 3 13:25 - 13:46  (00:21)
hermit      network     Tue Oct 3 13:23 - 13:55  (00:32)
wong        ftp         Tue Oct 3 13:21 - 13:56  (00:35)
perarl      network     Tue Oct 3 13:21 - 13:51  (00:30)
miller      ftp         Tue Oct 3 13:20 - 13:52  (00:32)
perkins     network     Tue Oct 3 13:20 - 13:26  (00:06)
cosmo       network     Tue Oct 3 13:19 - 13:59  (00:40)
casell      network     Tue Oct 3 13:17 - 13:59  (00:42)
botall      ftp         Tue Oct 3 13:16 - 13:58  (00:42)
brinker     network     Tue Oct 3 13:15 - 13:58  (00:43)
garlow      ftp         Tue Oct 3 13:13 - 13:56  (00:43)
saint       ftp         Tue Oct 3 13:10 - 13:48  (00:38)
mitchell    ftp         Tue Oct 3 13:06 - 13:28  (00:22)
hart        network     Tue Oct 3 13:05 - 13:58  (00:53)
brenso      ftp         Tue Oct 3 13:03 - 13:11  (00:08)
sylvan      ftp         Tue Oct 3 13:00 - 13:48  (00:48)
```

Notice that the output of this command lists the most recent logins and logouts first and the least recent logins and logouts last. This is because **last** searches backwards through the **/var/adm/wtmp** file. The command was run to produce an output of only 40 lines.

Here is an example of what your system administrator would see if he or she were to run the **lastb** command:

```
# lastb -10

castro     network     Tue Oct 3 12:03
preston    network     Tue Oct 3 11:58
smith      ttyp2       Tue Oct 3 11:56
cooper     ttyp1       Tue Oct 3 11:55
simms      network     Tue Oct 3 11:53
bileski    network     Tue Oct 3 11:51
moore      ftp         Tue Oct 3 11:50
vcup       ttyp9       Tue Oct 3 11:34
hroot      network     Tue Oct 3 11:33
lroot      network     Tue Oct 3 11:32
```

Notice that the output of this command lists the most recent login attempts first and the least recent login attempts last. This is because **lastb** searches backwards through the **/var/adm/btmp file**. Some of the names typed as part of these unsuccessful logins, such as *hroot* and *lroot*, were the user name (*root* in this case) typed incorrectly. The command was run to produce an output of only 10 lines.

I may cover some commands in too much detail for your liking and others in insufficient detail. If there is a command you wish to know more about you can use the on-line manual pages. By typing **man** followed by the name of the command you want to know more about the manual page for that command will be printed to your screen. Your system administrator decides which manual pages are loaded on your system. It is possible for you to attempt to view the manual pages for a command that has not been loaded on your system. In addition, there is an HP application called LaserROM which is a CD-ROM that contains many of the HP manuals. You may want to ask your system administrator if you have LaserROM and, if so, to give you access to it.

In the next chapter I'll cover the HP-UX file system layout. This will include a figure showing the hierarchy of the HP-UX file system, explanations of the contents of the most important directories, and a description of the different file types.

Chapter 3

The HP-UX File System

HP-UX File Types

A file is a means by which information is stored on an HP-UX system. The commands you issue, the applications you use, the data you store, and the devices you access such as printers and keyboard are all contained in files. This is one of the aspects of HP-UX that makes it both simple and complex; simple because you know everything out there is a file, complex because the contents of a file could be anything ranging from simple data you can read, to a device file that is created by your system administrator with a unique set of commands.

Every file on the system has a file name. The operating system takes care of all file system related tasks; you just need to know the name of the file and how to use it. The file types we will look at are:

- Text Files

- Data Files

- Source Code Files

- Executable Files

- Shell Programs

- Links

- Device Files

Text Files

What could be simpler than a file that contains characters, just like the ones you're now reading in this chapter? These ASCII characters are letters and numerals that represent the work you perform. If, for instance, you use an HP-UX editor to create an electronic mail message or a letter, you are creating a text file in most cases. Here is an example of part of a text file:

```
*                                                              *
 *                                                            *
  *                   HP LaserROM/UX                         *
   *                   README File                          *
     * * * * * * * * * * * * * * * * * * * * * * * * * * * * * * *
```

```
This version of HP LaserROM/UX can only be installed and run
on HP-UX Operating System Release 10.x or better.

The graphical user interface of HP LaserROM/UX requires the X
Window System version 11, Release 5 or later.
```

This text file is easy to read, has no data or other information in it, and can be easily modified.

Data Files

A file that contains data used by one of your applications is a data file. If you use a sophisticated desktop publishing tool such as FrameMaker to write a book, you create data files that FrameMaker® uses. These data files contain data, which you can usually read, and formatting information, which you can sometimes read but is usually hidden from you. If your HP-UX installation uses a database program, then you may have data files which you can partially read.

Source Code File

A source code file is a text file that contains information related to a programming language such as C, C++, Pascal, Fortran, and so on. When a programmer develops a source code file, they create a file that conforms to the naming convention of the program language being used, such as adding a ".c" to the end of the file if creating a C program.

The following is an example of a C source code file:

```
/* this is K & R sort program */

# include <stdio.h>
# include <stdlib.h>

        int N;
        int v[1000000];        /* v is array to be sorted */
        int left = 0;          /* left pointer */
        int right;
        int swapcount, comparecount = 0;
                               /* count swaps and compares*/
        int i, j, t;
        char print;
        char pr_incr_sorts;


main()

{
    printf("Enter number of numbers to sort : ");
    scanf("%10d", &N);                    /* 10d used for a BIG input */
    printf ("\n");                        /* select type of input to sort */

    printf("Enter rand(1), in-order(2), or reverse order (3)   sort : ");
    scanf("%2d", &type);
```

```
    printf ("\n");                          /* select type of input to sort */

    if (type == 3)
                for (i=0; i<N; ++i)         /* random          */
                    v[i] = (N - i);

    else if (type == 2)
                for (i=0; i<N; ++i)
                    v[i]= (i + 1);           /* in order        */

    else if (type == 1)
                for (i=0; i<N; ++i)
                    v[i]=rand();             /* reverse order */
    fflush(stdin);
    printf("Do you want to see the numbers before sorting (y or n)? : ");
    scanf("%c", &print);
    printf ("\n");                          /* View unsorted numbers?  */
    if (print == 'y')
      {
            printf ("\n");
         for (i=0; i<N; ++i)
            printf("a[%2d]= %2d\n", i, v[i]);
            printf ("\n");
      }


      fflush(stdin);
      printf("Do you want to see the array at each step as it sorts? (y or n)? : ");
      scanf("%c", &pr_incr_sorts);
      printf ("\n");                        /* View incremental sorts?  */

       right = N-1;                         /* right pointer          */

                qsort(v, left, right);




      {
       fflush(stdin);
       printf ("Here is the sorted list of %2d items\n", N);
            printf ("\n");
        for (i=0; i<N; ++i)
            printf ("%2d\n ", v[i]);
            printf ("\n");
            printf ("\n");                  /* print sorted list      */
                }
                printf ("number of swaps = %2d\n ", swapcount);
                printf ("number of compares = %2d\n ", comparecount);
       }

/* qsort function */

        void qsort( v, left, right)
                    int v[], left, right;
      {
                int i, last;
                if (left > right)
                 return;


                swap(v, left, (left + right)/2);
                last = left;
                for (i=left+1; i <= right; i++)
                {
                    comparecount = ++comparecount;
                      if (v[i] < v[left])
                    swap(v, ++last, i);
                }
                swap(v, left, last);
                qsort(v, left, last-1);
                qsort(v, last+1, right);
                }
```

```
                       /* swap function  */


                   swap(v, i, j)
                       int v[], i, j;

                       {int temp;
                          swapcount = swapcount++;
                          temp = v[i];
                          v[i] = v[j];
                          v[j] = temp;


      if (pr_incr_sorts == 'y')
         {
                       printf("Incremental sort of array = ");
            printf ("\n");
            for (i=0; i<N; ++i)
               printf("a[%2d]= %2d\n", i, v[i]);
               printf ("\n");
         }
      }
```

Executable Files

Executable files are compiled programs that can be run. You can't read executable files and you'll typically get a bunch of errors, unreadable characters, and beeps from your HP-UX system when you try to look at one of these. It is also possible you will lose your screen settings and cause other problems.

You don't have to go far in HP-UX to find executable files, they are everywhere. Many of the HP-UX commands you issue are executable files that you can't read. In addition, if you are developing programs on your system you are creating your own executables.

Here is an example of what you see if you attempt to send an executable to the screen:

```
unknown/etc/ttytyperunknown<@=>|<@=>|:unknown<@=>
callocLINESCOLUMNSunknownPackaged for
argbad aftger%3
parmnumber missing <@=>|<@=>|:
@ @ 3### @@@A:2TTO|>@#<|2X00R
EraseKillOOPS<@=>|<@=>|:
<@=>|<@=>|:
<@=>|<@=>|:<@=>|ATOO<@=>|:<@=>|<@=>|:<@=>|<@=>|:<@=>|<@=>|:
```

Shell Programs

A shell program is both a file you can run to perform a task and a file that you can read. So yes, even though you can run this file because it is executable, you can also read it. I'm going to describe shell programming in more detail in an upcoming chapter.

I consider shell programming to be an important skill for every user to have. I'll spend some time going over the basics of shell programming. Some of the background I'm about to cover relating to file types and permissions is important when it comes to shell programming, so this is important information for you to understand.

Here is an example of part of a shell program that sets up some of your HP VUE environment when you log in:

```
# Check if login script contains non-comment to "VUE"
# If it does, assume it's VUE safe, and set VUESOURCEPROFILE
# to true.
if [ "${SHELL:-}" -a -d "${HOME:-}; then
  case ${SHELL##*/} in
   sh | ksh ) shellprofile="$HOME/.profile" ;;
        csh ) shellprofile="$HOME/.login" ;;
          * ) shellprofile="" ;;

  esac
  if [[ -r "$shellprofile"]] ; then
    [ 'grep -c '^[^#:].*VUE' $shellprofile' !=0 ] &&
      VUERESOURCEPROFILE="true"
 fi
fi

# Place customization code beyond this point.

PATH="$PATH:/usr/local/bin:/usr/sbin:$HOME:."
export PATH

mesg y

umask 022
```

The shell program is text you can read and modify if indeed you have permissions to do so. In addition to programming information, shell programs contain comments indicated by lines beginning with a #.

Links

A link is a pointer to a file stored elsewhere on the system. Instead of having two or more copies of a file on your system, you can link to a file that already exists on your system.

One particularly useful way links have been used in HP-UX is related to new releases of the operating system. The locations of files sometimes change going from one release to another, and rather than learn all the new locations there are links produced from the old location to the new one. When you run a command using the old location, the link points to the new location.

Links are also useful for centralizing files. If a set of identical files has to be updated often, it is easier to link to a central file and update it rather than have to update several copies of the file in several different locations.

Device Files

Device files, sometimes called device special files, contain information about the hardware connected to your system. Because device special files are associated with system administration functions they are usually not covered much in user, as opposed to system administration, material. I think it should be otherwise. It is very frustrating for a user to want to write a file to a floppy disk or a tape and not have any idea how to access a device file. I'll cover some use of device files so you are not completely in the dark in this area.

Devices on your system can often be accessed with different device files. A disk, for instance, can be accessed with either a block device file or a character device file. Most of this is the responsibility of your system administrator; however, when you attempt to determine the file type you may encounter special files of different types such as character and block.

There are other types of files on your system as well, but for the purposes of getting started with HP-UX, the file types I will describe supply sufficient background to get you started.

The file Command

The **file** command is used to determine the file type. This command is useful because the name of a file does not always indicate its file type. The following examples perform a long listing of a file to provide some background information on the file, and then the **file** command is run to show the file type. I don't cover the command used to list files until the next chapter, but I include it in these examples:

Text File

(Described by the **file** command as *ascii text.*)

```
# ll  .mosaic-global-history
-rw-r--r--   1 201      users       587 Dec 22  1994 .mosaic-global-history
```

```
# file   .mosaic-global-history
.mosaic-global-history: ascii text
#
```

Data File

(Described by the **file** command as *data*.)

```
# ll Static.dat
-rw-r--r--   1 201        users       235874 Aug 26  1993 Static.dat
# file Static.dat
Static.dat:      data
#
```

Source Code File

(Described by the **file** command as *c program text*.)

```
# ll krsort.c
-rwxrwxrwx   1 201        users       3234 Nov 16  1992 krsort.c
# file krsort.c
krsort.c:        c program text
#
```

Executable File

(Described by the **file** command as *shared executable*.)

```
# ll krsort
-rwxr-xr-x  1 201        users       34592 Nov 16  1992 krsort
# file krsort
krsort:          PA-RISC1.1 shared executable dynamically linked -not stripped
#
```

Shell Program

(Described by the **file** command as *commands text*.)

```
# ll llsum
-rwxrwxrwx   1 root      sys          1267 Feb 23  1993 llsum
# file llsum
llsum:          commands text
#
```

Link

(The link is not referenced by the **file** command, this is shown as a *shared executable dynamically linked*. The reference to *dynamically linked* does not mean this is a link.)

```
# ll /usr/bin/ar
lr-xr-xr-t   1 root      sys            15 Mar 23  1995 ar -> /usr/ccs/bin/ar
# file /usr/bin/ar
/usr/bin/ar:       s800 shared executable dynamically linked
#
```

Block Device File

(Described by the **file** command as *block special*.)

```
# ll /dev/dsk/c0t1d0
brw-r--r--   1 bin      sys         31 0x001000 Apr 17  1995 /dev/dsk/c0t1d0
# file /dev/dsk/c0t1d0
/dev/dsk/c0t1d0:     block special (31/4096)
#
```

Character Device File

(Described by the **file** command as *character special*.)

```
# ll /dev/rdsk/c0t1d0
crw-r-----   1 root      sys       188 0x001000 Mar 23  1995 /dev/rdsk/c0t1d0
# file /dev/rdsk/c0t1d0
/dev/rdsk/c0t1d0:        character special (188/4096)
#
```

File System Layout

Before I begin talking about the file system layout, it is important for
you to know that there is not necessarily a single file system. Your system administrator may have set up a variety of file system types on your
system. As a beginning user you don't care too much about the different
types of file systems; however, before proceeding to the file system layout, let me briefly cover some of the different file system types. Your
system administrator cares a lot about the different file system types
because the commands he or she issues allow them to specify the option
"-F" followed by the file system type. Some of the commands that support this new option are **dcopy**, **fsck**, **mksf**, **mount**, **newfs**, and others,
some of which you may need to know as an advanced user if you are
going to perform system administration in the future. Here is a brief
description of four file system types supported by HP-UX:

• High Performance File System (HFS) is HP's
version of the UNIX File System. This is the
most common file system and the one used in
most of the examples.

• CD-ROM File System (CDFS) is used when
you mount a CD-ROM. A CD-ROM is read-
only so you can't write to it.

• Network File System (NFS) is a way of
accessing files on other systems on the network
from your local system. An NFS mounted file

system looks as though it is local to your system even though it is located on another system.

• Loopback File System (LOFS) allows you to have the same file system in multiple places.

• VxFs is an extent, based Journal File System that supports fast file system recovery and on-line features such as backup.

I am going to cover only the HP-UX 10.x file system layout in this chapter. The 10.x file system layout is derived from the OSF/1 layout, which is based on the AT&T SVR4 layout.

You'll be very happy to read that all of the file system related information in this section applies to both HP 9000 Series 800 and Series 700 systems (servers and workstations respectively.) This means that you can take the information in this section and apply it to all HP 9000 systems.

Figure 3-1 is a high level depiction of the HP-UX 10.x file system.

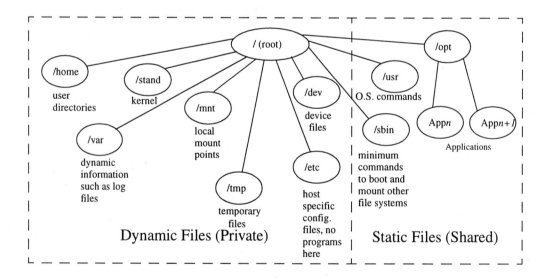

Figure 3-1   HP-UX 10.x File System Layout

Here are some of the more important features of the 10.x file system layout:

• Files and directories are organized by category. The two most obvious categories that appear in Figure 3-1 are static vs. dynamic files. There are also other categories such as executable, configuration, data files, and so on. The static files are also labeled "shared" because other hosts on the network may share these. The directories **/usr, /sbin**, and **/opt** are shared directories.

• The operating system and applications are kept separate from one another. Application vendors don't care where their applications are loaded; that is up to you. But to a system administrator it is highly desirable to keep applications separate from the operating system, so you don't inadvertently have application files overwriting operating system files. In addition, if applications are loaded in a separate area they are "modular," meaning a system administrator can add, remove, and modify them without affecting the operating system or other applications. Applications are kept in the **/opt** directory.

• Intrasystem files are kept in a separate area from intersystem, or network accessible, files. **/usr** and **/sbin** are shared operating system directories. There is no host specific information in these two directories. **/etc** is used to hold the hostspecific configuration files.

• Executable files are kept separate from system configuration files so that the executables may be shared among hosts. Having the configuration files separate from the programs that use them also means that updates to the operating system won't affect the configuration files.

I'll provide descriptions of some of the most important directories for HP-UX 10.x.

/ This is the root directory, which is the base of the file system's hierarchical tree structure. A directory is logically viewed as being part of **/**. Regardless of the disk on which a directory or logical volume is stored, it is logically viewed as a part of the root hierarchy.

/dev Contains hostspecific devices files.

/etc Contains host-specific system and application configuration files. The information in this directory is important to the operation of the system and is of a permanent nature. There are also additional configuration directories below **/etc**. There are two **/etc** subdirectories of particular interest:

/etc/rc.config.d contains configuration data files for startup and shutdown programs.

/etc/opt contains host specific application configuration data.

/export This is used for diskless file sharing only. Servers export root directories for networked clients.

/home Users' home directories are located here. Since the data stored in users' home directories will be modified often, you can expect this directory to grow in size.

/lost+found This is the lost files directory. Here you will find files that are in use but are not associated with a directory. These files typically become "lost" as a result of a system crash that caused the link between the physical information on the disk and the logical directory to be severed. The program **fsck**, which is run at the time of boot, finds these files and places them in the **lost+found** directory.

/mnt This directory is reserved as a mount point for local file systems. You can either mount directly to **/mnt** or have **/mnt** subdirectories as mount points such as **/mnt1**, **/mnt2**, **/mnt3**, etc.

/net Name reserved as mount points for remote file systems.

/opt The directory under which applications are installed. As a rule, application vendors never specify a particular location for their applications to be installed. Now, with **/opt**, we have a standard directory under which applications should be installed. This is an organizational improvement for system administrators, because we can now expect applications to be loaded under **/opt** and the application name.

/sbin   Contains commands and scripts used to boot, shut down, and fix file system mounting problems. **/sbin** is available when a system boots because it contains commands required to bring up a system.

/stand   Contains kernel configuration and binary files that are required to bring up a system. Two significant files contained in this directory are the **system** and **vmunix** (kernel) files.

/tmp   This is a free-for-all directory where any user can *temporarily store* files. Because of the loose nature of this directory, it should not be used to store anything important, and users should know that whatever they have stored in **/tmp** can be deleted without notice. In 10.x, application working files should go in **/var/tmp** or **/var/opt/appname**, not in **/tmp**.

/usr   Most of the HP-UX operating system is contained in **/usr**. Included in this directory are commands, libraries, and documentation. There are a limited number of subdirectories that can appear in **/usr**. Here is a list of **/usr** subdirectories:

/usr/bin - Common utilities and applications are stored here.

/usr/ccs - Tools and libraries used to generate C programs are stored here.

/usr/conf - Static directory containing the sharable kernel build environment.

/usr/contrib - Contributed software directory.

/usr/include - Contains header files.

/usr/lib - Contains libraries and machine dependent databases.

/usr/newconfig - Contains default operating system data files such as those found in **/etc/ newconfig** in HP-UX 10.x, although the directory structure of **/usr/newconfig** is different than that of **/etc/newconfig**.

/usr/old - Old files from an operating system update will be stored here.

/usr/sbin - System administration commands are in this directory, including many that had been in **/etc** in HP-UX 9.x.

/usr/share - Contains files that are architecture independent and can be shared.

/usr/share/man - Directory for manual pages.

/var   Holds files that are primarily temporary. Files such as log files, which are frequently deleted and modified, are stored here. Think of this as a directory of "variable" size. Files that an application or command create at runtime should be placed in this directory, including log and spool files. There may, however, be some applications which store state information in **/var**.

/var/adm - Directory for administrative files, log files, and databases such as kernel crash dumps will be stored here.

/var/adm/crash - Kernel crash dumps will be placed here.

/var/adm/sw - Software Distributor log files, etc.

/usr/var/cron - Log files for **cron**.

/var/mail - Incoming mail messages are kept here.

/var/opt - Application runtime files, such as log files, for applications mounted in **/opt** will be stored in **/var/opt** under the application name.

/var/spool -Spool files, such as those in **/usr/spool** in HP-UX 10.x, are stored here.

Figure 3-2 is an HP VUE file manager window showing the top-level file system with the **sbin** directory selected.

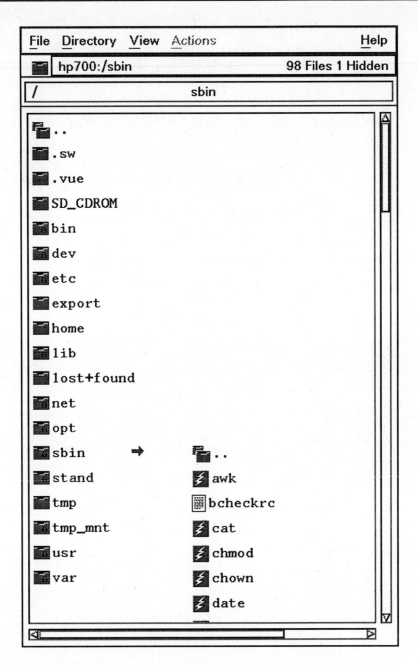

Figure 3-2   HP VUE File Manager Window Showing HP-UX 10.x File System

In the next chapter I'll cover HP-UX file system commands and file permissions. This will include an overview of how permissions are assigned so you can easily determine what files you can read, write, and execute. I'll then cover the **ls** command and wild cards.

Chapter 4

Permissions, the ls Command, and File Name Expansion and Wild Cards

Permissions

The best place to begin discussing permissions is by issuing the **ls** command, which lists the contents of directories. Permissions is the means by which files and directories are made secure on your HP-UX system. Since HP-UX is multiuser there are potentially thousands of users who could be accessing the files on a system. Permissions controls who has access to what files.

Here is an example **ls -l** command and output:

```
$ ls -l sort
-rwxr-x--x   1 marty      users      120 Jul 26 10:20 sort
```

Issuing this command has produced a lot of information relating to a file called **sort**. Let's begin to understand what this listing has produced by analyzing the first set of characters (-rwxr-x--x). This set of characters is made up of four distinct fields, as shown in Figure 4-1.

49

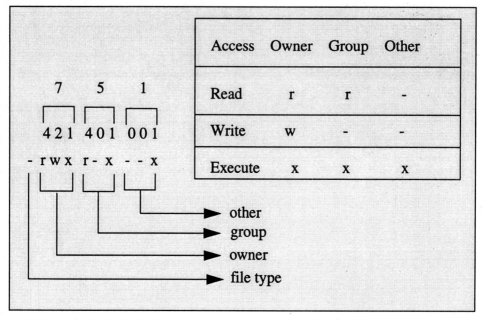

Figure 4-1   Permissions For File **sort**

This first character in this group is related to the file type. I covered some file types earlier, but the **ls -l** command will not analyze files to the same level of detail. Among the types of files **ls -l** will list are shown in Figure 4-2.

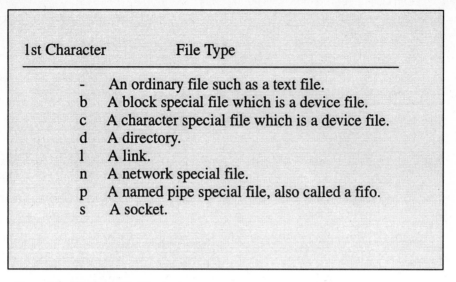

1st Character	File Type
-	An ordinary file such as a text file.
b	A block special file which is a device file.
c	A character special file which is a device file.
d	A directory.
l	A link.
n	A network special file.
p	A named pipe special file, also called a fifo.
s	A socket.

Figure 4-2   File Types of ls Command

For every file on the system, HP-UX supports three classes of access:

- User access (u). Access granted to the owner of the file.

- Group access (g). Access granted to members of the same group as the owner of the file.

- Other access (o). Access granted to everyone else.

These access rights are defined by the position of read (r), write (w), and execute (x) when the long listing command is issued. For the long listing (**ls -l**) issued earlier, you see the permissions in Table 4-1.

Table 4-1   Long Listing Permissions For The File **sort**

Access	User Access	Group Access	Other
Read	r	r	-
Write	w	-	-
Execute	x	x	x

Permissions are not granted where a "-" appears. In addition, there are other permissions such as s, S, t, and T which I won't cover at this time.

You can see that access rights are arranged in groups of three. There are three groups of permissions with three access levels each. The owner, in this case *marty*, has read, write, and execute permissions on the file. Anyone in the group *users* is permitted read and execute access to the file. *other* is permitted only execute access of the file.

The definitions of read, write, and execute differ somewhat for files and directories. Here is what you can do if you have read, write, and execute permissions for files:

read   You have permission to read the file.

write   You have permission to change and to write the   file.

execute   You can run, or execute, the program.

Here is what you can do if you have read, write, and execute permissions for directories:

read   You can list the contents of the directory.

write   You can create files in the directory, delete files in the directory, and create subdirectories in the directory.

execute You can change to this directory using the **cd** command, which we'll cover shortly.

We will cover permissions again when the **chmod** command is described.

Absolute and Relative Path Names

We have already covered two topics that can serve as the basis for a discussion of absolute and relative path names: some important directories on the system and user login. If we go back to the user **denise** and look at the way some of her files may be organized, we can get to the bottom of relative and absolute path names quickly.

The HP-UX file system covered in Chapter 3 showed a hierarchy. In this hierarchy there was the root (/) directory at the top, and files and directories below root. The two means by which you can traverse this hierarchy to get to a "lower" point are with absolute path names and relative path names. Let's take a closer look at the files and directories **denise** may have in her user area.

First of all we'll assume that **denise** has many files. This is one of the things users do - create files. In addition, your system administrator has provided several default files for purposes such as defining your user environment after login (we'll get into this in a lot more detail in upcoming chapters). **denise** probably has many files under her user area and subdirectories as well. Her user area may look something like that shown in Figure 4-3.

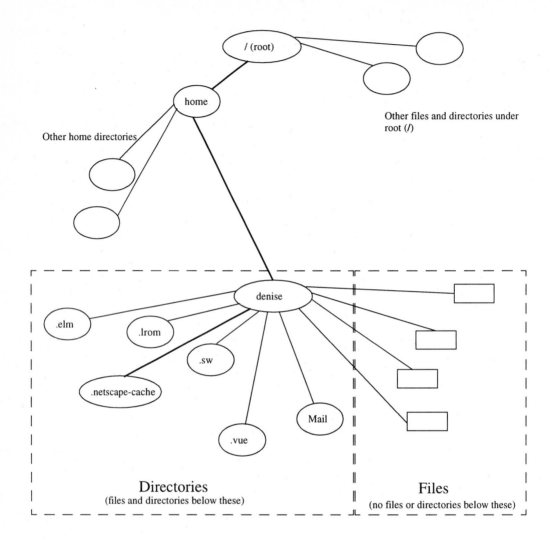

Figure 4-3   Home Directory for **denise**

Most users will have their home directory under **/home** (and who said UNIX doesn't make any sense). If you wanted to get to a subdirectory of **denise** using an absolute path name you would traverse the hierarchy using the complete path. To get to the directory **.netscape-cache** under **denise** you could view the absolute path as shown in Figure 4-4.

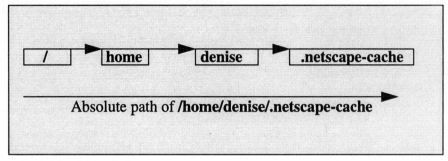

Figure 4-4   Absolute Path

You are progressing from root (**/**), to **home**, to **denise**, and finally to the directory **.netscape-cache**. The change directory (**cd**) command you would issue looks like the following:

```
$ cd /home/denise/.netscape-cache
```

This is an absolute path because it starts at root and progresses through the hierarchy. No matter what directory you are currently working in, even if it is **.netscape-cache**, you could use the absolute path name. In many cases, however, you may not need to issue an absolute path name. You may be so close to the file or directory you wish to get access to that the absolute path would be a waste of time for you. If, for instance, you are already in **/home/denise**, then you could change to **.netscape-cache** using a relative path name easily:

```
$ cd .netscape-cache
```

The relative path name is shorted because you don't begin it with a slash (/) that brings you back up to the top of their hierarchy to work your way down. Instead, you are starting at some point in the file system hierarchy, such as **/home/denise**, and entering a path relative to that directory such as **/home/denise**.

The ls Command

The **ls** command brings about a lot to discuss. I haven't yet described the options to **ls,** yet we have already used the **-l** option as part of the permissions discussion in this chapter as well as the **file** command discussion in Chapter 3. The best way to cover the most important options to **ls** is to show examples. I will do just that in the upcoming description of the **ls** command.

ls

The following is an example of **ls** without any options other than the directory to list:

```
# ls /home/densie

27247b.exe
410pt1.exe
410pt2.exe
41ndir.exe
41nds1.exe
41nds4.exe
41nwad.exe
41rtr2.exe
HPDA1.EXE
Mail
N3212B6.EXE
SCSI4S.EXE
clean
clean2
clean3
content.exe
dsenh.exe
eg1
eg2
en0316bz.exe
en0316tb.exe
explore.exe
flexi_cd.exe
fred.h
```

```
hal.c
hpdl0117.exe
hpdlinst.txt
hpux.patches
j2577a.exe
ja95up.exe
msie10.exe
n32e12n.exe
nfs197.exe
pass.sb
plusdemo.exe
ps4x03.exe
psg
quik_res.exe
rclock.exe
rkhelp.exe
roni.mak
sb.txt
smsup2.exe
softinit.remotesoftcm
srvpr.exe
steve.h
target.exe
tcp41a.exe
tnds2.exe
upgrade.exe
whoon
win95app.exe
total 46718
```

Which of these are files? Which are directories? Have all of the
entries been listed? There are many options to **ls** that will answer these
questions.

There is not a lot of information reported as a result of having
issued this command. **ls** lists the contents of the directory specified, or
the current working directory if no directory is specified.

ls -a

To list all of the entries of a directory you would use the **-a** option. Files
that begin with a "." are called hidden files and are not usually listed with
ls. The following example shows the output of **ls -a**:

```
$ ls -a /home/denise

.Xauthority
.cshrc
.elm
.exrc
.fmrc.orig
.glancerc
.gpmhp
.history
```

```
.login
.lrom
.mailrc
.netscape-bookmarks.html
.netscape-cache
.netscape-cookies
.netscape-history
.netscape-newsgroups-news.spry.com
.netscape-newsgroups-newsserv.hp.com
.netscape-preferences
.newsrc-news.spry.com
.newsrc-newsserv.hp.com
.profile
.rhosts
.sh_history
.softbuildrc
.softinit.orig
.sw
.vue
.vueprofile
.xinitrc
.xsession
27247b.exe
410pt1.exe
410pt2.exe
41ndir.exe
41nds1.exe
41nds4.exe
41nwad.exe
41rtr2.exe
HPDA1.EXE
Mail
N3212B6.EXE
SCSI4S.EXE
clean
clean2
clean3
content.exe
dsenh.exe
eg1
eg2
en0316bz.exe
en0316tb.exe
explore.exe
flexi_cd.exe
fred.h
hal.c
hpdl0117.exe
hpdlinst.txt
hpux.patches
j2577a.exe
ja95up.exe
msie10.exe
n32e12n.exe
nfs197.exe
pass.sb
plusdemo.exe
ps4x03.exe
psg
quik_res.exe
rclock.exe
rkhelp.exe
roni.mak
sb.txt
smsup2.exe
softinit.remotesoftcm
srvpr.exe
steve.h
target.exe
tcp41a.exe
tnds2.exe
upgrade.exe
whoon
win95app.exe
total 46718
```

Notice that this output includes hidden files, those that begin with a
".", as well as all other files listed with just **ls**. These did not appear when
ls was issued without the **-a** option.

ls -l

To list all information about the contents of directory you would use the
-l option to **ls** as shown in the following example (some of these file
names were shortened to fit on the page):

```
$ ls -l /home/denise

-rw-------   1 denise   users        98 Oct  6 09:19 .Xauthority
-r--r--r--   1 denise   users       814 May 19 10:10 .cshrc
drwx------   2 denise   users      1024 Jul 31 18:48 .elm
-r--r--r--   1 denise   users       347 May 19 10:10 .exrc
-rwxrwxrwx   1 denise   users       170 Jun  6 14:20 .fmrc.orig
-rw-------   1 denise   users        97 Jun 12 18:59 .glancerc
-rw-------   1 denise   users     17620 Sep 21 16:11 .gpmhp
-rwxr-xr-x   1 denise   users       391 Sep 19 09:55 .history
-r--r--r--   1 denise   users       341 May 19 10:10 .login
drwx--x--x   2 denise   users      1024 Jul 31 18:48 .lrom
-rw-r--r--   1 denise   users       768 Jul 28 12:54 .mailrc
-rw-------   1 denise   users      1450 Oct  6 13:58 .netscape-bookmarks.html
drwx------   2 denise   users     10240 Oct 10 15:24 .netscape-cache
-rw-------   1 denise   users        91 Sep 18 14:16 .netscape-cookies
-rw-------   1 denise   users     43906 Oct 10 15:32 .netscape-history
-rw-r--r--   1 denise   users       566 Aug 25 14:36 .netscape--news.spry.com
-rw-------   1 denise   users     46514 Jun 28 12:35 .netscape-.hp.com
-rw-------   1 denise   users      1556 Sep 28 15:02 .netscape-preferences
-rw-------   1 denise   users       104 Jul 11 11:01 .newsrc-news.spry.com
-rw-r--r--   1 denise   users       223 Sep 26 13:26 .newsrc-newv.hp.com
-r--r--r--   1 denise   users       446 May 19 10:10 .profile
-rw-------   1 denise   users        21 Jul  6 13:21 .rhosts
-rw-------   1 denise   users      2328 Oct 10 15:22 .sh_history
-rw-r--r--   1 denise   users      1052 Sep 22 15:00 .softbuildrc
-rwxrwxrwx   1 denise   users       161 Jul 11 12:19 .softinit.orig
drwxr-xr-x   3 denise   users      1024 Aug 31 15:44 .sw
drwxr-xr-x   7 denise   users      1024 Sep 26 11:14 .vue
-rwxr-xr-x   1 denise   users      8705 Jul  7 12:04 .vueprofile
-rw-------   1 denise   users        23 Jun  2 15:01 .xinitrc
-rwxr-xr-x   1 denise   users     11251 May 19 10:41 .xsession
-rw-r--r--   1 denise   users    611488 Oct  3 12:00 27247b.exe
-rw-r--r--   1 denise   users    114119 Sep 29 12:49 410pt1.exe
-rw-r--r--   1 denise   users    136979 Sep 29 12:53 410pt2.exe
-rw-r--r--   1 denise   users    173978 Sep 29 12:40 41ndir.exe
-rw-r--r--   1 denise   users    363315 Sep 29 12:52 41nds1.exe
-rw-r--r--   1 denise   users    527524 Sep 29 12:57 41nds4.exe
-rw-r--r--   1 denise   users   1552513 Sep 29 12:50 41nwad.exe
-rw-r--r--   1 denise   users    853424 Sep 29 12:24 41rtr2.exe
-rw-r--r--   1 denise   users   1363011 Sep 20 12:20 HPDA1.EXE
drwx------   2 denise   users        24 Jul 31 18:48 Mail
-rw-r--r--   1 denise   users   1787840 Aug 31 09:35 N3212B6.EXE
-rw-r--r--   1 denise   users     13543 Sep 23 09:46 SCSI4S.EXE
```

```
-rw-r--r--    1 denise    users       28395 Aug 30 15:07 cabview.exe
-rwx--x--x    1 denise    users          66 Jun  8 17:40 clean
-rwx--x--x    1 denise    users          99 Jun 20 17:44 clean2
-rwx--x--x    1 denise    users          66 Jun 20 17:51 clean3
-rw-r--r--    1 denise    users       15365 Aug 30 15:07 content.exe
-rw-r--r--    1 denise    users      713313 Sep 29 12:56 dsenh.exe
-rwx------    1 denise    users         144 Aug 14 17:10 eg1
-rwx------    1 denise    users         192 Aug 15 12:13 eg2
-rw-r--r--    1 denise    users      667890 Sep 20 12:41 en0316bz.exe
-rw-r--r--    1 denise    users      641923 Sep 20 12:42 en0316tb.exe
-rw-r--r--    1 denise    users        6251 Aug 30 15:07 explore.exe
-rw-r--r--    1 denise    users       23542 Aug 30 15:08 flexi_cd.exe
-rw-r--r--    1 denise    users          30 Aug 14 17:02 fred.h
-rw-r--r--    1 denise    users           0 Aug 14 17:24 hal.c
-rw-r--r--    1 denise    users      895399 Sep 20 12:32 hpd10117.exe
-rw-r--r--    1 denise    users       14135 Sep 20 12:39 hpdlinst.txt
-rw-------    1 denise    users        2943 Jun 19 14:42 hpux.patches
-rw-r--r--    1 denise    users      680279 Sep 20 12:26 j2577a.exe
-rw-r--r--    1 denise    users      930728 Sep 20 15:16 ja95up.exe
-rw-r--r--    1 denise    users       53575 Oct 10 10:37 mbox
-rw-r--r--    1 denise    users     1097728 Aug 30 15:03 msie10.exe
-rw-r--r--    1 denise    users     1790376 Sep 18 14:32 n32e12n.exe
-rw-r--r--    1 denise    users     1393835 Sep 29 12:59 nfs197.exe
-rw-------    1 denise    users         977 Jul  3 14:25 pass.sb
-rw-r--r--    1 denise    users     1004544 Aug 30 15:00 plusdemo.exe
-rw-r--r--    1 denise    users      229547 Sep 29 12:27 ps4x03.exe
-rwxr--r--    1 denise    users         171 Aug  9 13:43 psg
-rw-r--r--    1 denise    users       16645 Aug 30 15:08 quik_res.exe
-rw-r--r--    1 denise    users       14544 Aug 30 15:08 rclock.exe
-rw-r--r--    1 denise    users     2287498 Aug 30 15:12 rkhelp.exe
-rw-r--r--    1 denise    users           0 Aug 15 12:10 roni.mak
-rw-r--r--    1 denise    users        1139 Sep 28 10:35 sb.txt
-rw-r--r--    1 denise    users      569855 Sep 29 12:55 smsup2.exe
-rw-------    1 root      sys          161 Jul 11 12:18 softinit.remotesoftcm
-rw-r--r--    1 denise    users          39 Sep 29 12:48 srvpr.exe
-rw-r--r--    1 denise    users          38 Aug 15 12:14 steve.h
-rw-r--r--    1 denise    users       14675 Aug 30 15:08 target.exe
-rw-r--r--    1 denise    users      229630 Sep 29 12:54 tcp41a.exe
-rw-r--r--    1 denise    users     1954453 Sep 29 12:26 tnds2.exe
-rw-r--r--    1 denise    users      364270 Sep 23 09:50 upgrade.exe
-rwx-----x    1 denise    users          88 Aug  9 13:43 whoon
-rw-r--r--    1 denise    users      191495 Aug 30 15:00 win95app.exe
total 46718
```

Because I find this to be the most commonly used option with the **ls** command I'll describe each of the fields produced by **ls -l**. I'll use the earlier example of the **ls -l** command, which showed only one file when describing the fields.

```
$ ls -l sort
-rwxr-x--x    1 marty      users         120 Jul 26 10:20 sort
```

The first field is the access rights of the file which I covered in the last section. The *owner* has read, write, and execute permissions on the file. The *group* has read and execute permissions on the file. *other* has execute permissions.

The second field is the link count. This lists how many files are symbolically linked to the file. We will get into the details of the **ln** command used to link files later. In this case the link count is 1, which means only this file is linked to itself. For directories, such as **.vue** shown below, the number of subdirectories is shown rather than the link count. This number includes one for the directory itself as well as one for the parent directory. This means that there are a total of five directories below **.vue** .

```
drwxr-x--x    7 denise       users    1024 Jul 26 10:20 .vue
```

The subdirectories below **/home/denise/.vue are:**

> **/home/denise/.vue/Desktop**
> **/home/denise/.vue/apps**
> **/home/denise/.vue/palettes**
> **/home/denise/.vue/sessions**
> **/home/denise/.vue/types**

These five subdirectories plus the directory itself and the parent directory make a total of seven.

The third field lists the owner of the file. Your login name, such as **denise**, would be listed here. When you create a file your login name would be listed by default as the owner of the file.

The fourth field lists the group that the file belongs to. Groups were covered earlier.

The fifth field shows the size of the file. The file **sort** is 120 bytes in size.

The sixth field (which includes a date and time such as Jul 26 10:20) lists the date and time the file was created or last changed.

The seventh field lists the files and directories in alphabetical order. You'll first see the files that begin with a ".", then the files that begin with numbers, then the files that begin with upper case letters, and finally the files that begin with lower case letters. There are a lot of characters a file can begin with in HP-UX, so if you perform an **ls -l** and don't see the file you are looking for, it may appear at a different spot in the listing than you expected.

ls -i

To get information about the inode of a file you would use the **-i** option to **ls**. The following example includes both the **-i** and **-l** options to **ls**.

```
$ls -il /home/denise

137717 -rw-------   1 denise   users        98 Oct  6 09:19 .Xauthority
137623 -r--r--r--   1 denise   users       814 May 19 10:10 .cshrc
180815 drwx------   2 denise   users      1024 Jul 31 18:48 .elm
137624 -r--r--r--   1 denise   users       347 May 19 10:10 .exrc
137652 -rwxrwxrwx   1 denise   users       170 Jun  6 14:20 .fmrc.orig
137650 -rw-------   1 denise   users        97 Jun 12 18:59 .glancerc
137699 -rw-------   1 denise   users     17620 Sep 21 16:11 .gpmhp
137640 -rwxr-xr-x   1 denise   users       391 Sep 19 09:55 .history
137625 -r--r--r--   1 denise   users       341 May 19 10:10 .login
185607 drwx--x--x   2 denise   users      1024 Jul 31 18:48 .lrom
137642 -rw-r--r--   1 denise   users       768 Jul 28 12:54 .mailrc
137641 -rw-------   1 denise   users      1450 Oct  6 13:58 .netscaperks.html
179207 drwx------   2 denise   users     10240 Oct 10 15:24 .netscape-cache
137656 -rw-------   1 denise   users        91 Sep 18 14:16 .netscape-cookies
137635 -rw-------   1 denise   users     43906 Oct 10 15:32 .netscape-history
137645 -rw-r--r--   1 denise   users       566 Aug 25 14:36 .netscapes.spry.com
137646 -rw-------   1 denise   users     46514 Jun 28 12:35 .netsca
137634 -rw-------   1 denise   users      1556 Sep 28 15:02 .netscaperences
137637 -rw-------   1 denise   users       104 Jul 11 11:01 .newsrcws.spry.com
137633 -rw-r--r--   1 denise   users       223 Sep 26 13:26 .newsrc-hp.com
137626 -r--r--r--   1 denise   users       446 May 19 10:10 .profile
137649 -rw-------   1 denise   users        21 Jul  6 13:21 .rhosts
137694 -rw-------   1 denise   users      2328 Oct 10 15:22 .sh_history
137698 -rw-r--r--   1 denise   users      1052 Sep 22 15:00 .softbuildrc
137636 -rwxrwxrwx   1 denise   users       161 Jul 11 12:19 .softinit.orig
 33600 drwxr-xr-x   3 denise   users      1024 Aug 31 15:44 .sw
140820 drwxr-xr-x   7 denise   users      1024 Sep 26 11:14 .vue
137629 -rwxr-xr-x   1 denise   users      8705 Jul  7 12:04 .vueprofile
137648 -rw-------   1 denise   users        23 Jun  2 15:01 .xinitrc
137628 -rwxr-xr-x   1 denise   users     11251 May 19 10:41 .xsession
137715 -rw-r--r--   1 denise   users    611488 Oct  3 12:00 27247b.exe
137707 -rw-r--r--   1 denise   users    114119 Sep 29 12:49 410pt1.exe
137710 -rw-r--r--   1 denise   users    136979 Sep 29 12:53 410pt2.exe
137705 -rw-r--r--   1 denise   users    173978 Sep 29 12:40 41ndir.exe
137709 -rw-r--r--   1 denise   users    363315 Sep 29 12:52 41nds1.exe
137714 -rw-r--r--   1 denise   users    527524 Sep 29 12:57 41nds4.exe
137708 -rw-r--r--   1 denise   users   1552513 Sep 29 12:50 41nwad.exe
137696 -rw-r--r--   1 denise   users    853424 Sep 29 12:24 41rtr2.exe
137654 -rw-r--r--   1 denise   users   1363011 Sep 20 12:20 HPDA1.EXE
```

```
182429 drwx------   2 denise   users         24 Jul 31 18:48 Mail
137683 -rw-r--r--   1 denise   users    1787840 Aug 31 09:35 N3212B6.EXE
137702 -rw-r--r--   1 denise   users      13543 Sep 23 09:46 SCSI4S.EXE
137638 -rwx--x--x   1 denise   users         66 Jun  8 17:40 clean
137651 -rwx--x--x   1 denise   users         99 Jun 20 17:44 clean2
137632 -rwx--x--x   1 denise   users         66 Jun 20 17:51 clean3
137688 -rw-r--r--   1 denise   users      15365 Aug 30 15:07 content.exe
137713 -rw-r--r--   1 denise   users     713313 Sep 29 12:56 dsenh.exe
137667 -rwx------   1 denise   users        144 Aug 14 17:10 eg1
137671 -rwx------   1 denise   users        192 Aug 15 12:13 eg2
137662 -rw-r--r--   1 denise   users     667890 Sep 20 12:41 en0316bz.exe
137665 -rw-r--r--   1 denise   users     641923 Sep 20 12:42 en0316tb.exe
137689 -rw-r--r--   1 denise   users       6251 Aug 30 15:07 explore.exe
137690 -rw-r--r--   1 denise   users      23542 Aug 30 15:08 flexi_cd.exe
137670 -rw-r--r--   1 denise   users         30 Aug 14 17:02 fred.h
137673 -rw-r--r--   1 denise   users          0 Aug 14 17:24 hal.c
137660 -rw-r--r--   1 denise   users     895399 Sep 20 12:32 hpd10117.exe
137661 -rw-r--r--   1 denise   users      14135 Sep 20 12:39 hpdlinst.txt
137647 -rw-------   1 denise   users       2943 Jun 19 14:42 hpux.patches
137659 -rw-r--r--   1 denise   users     680729 Sep 20 12:26 j2577a.exe
137697 -rw-r--r--   1 denise   users     930728 Sep 20 15:16 ja95up.exe
137684 -rw-r--r--   1 denise   users    1097728 Aug 30 15:03 msie10.exe
137658 -rw-r--r--   1 denise   users    1790376 Sep 18 14:32 n32e12n.exe
137643 -rw-r--r--   1 denise   users    1393835 Sep 29 12:59 nfs197.exe
137639 -rw-------   1 denise   users        977 Jul  3 14:25 pass.sb
137664 -rw-r--r--   1 denise   users    1004544 Aug 30 15:00 plusdemo.exe
137704 -rw-r--r--   1 denise   users     229547 Sep 29 12:27 ps4x03.exe
137666 -rwxr--r--   1 denise   users        171 Aug  9 13:43 psg
137691 -rw-r--r--   1 denise   users      16645 Aug 30 15:08 quik_res.exe
137692 -rw-r--r--   1 denise   users      14544 Aug 30 15:08 rclock.exe
137693 -rw-r--r--   1 denise   users    2287498 Aug 30 15:12 rkhelp.exe
137669 -rw-r--r--   1 denise   users          0 Aug 15 12:10 roni.mak
137657 -rw-r--r--   1 denise   users       1139 Sep 28 10:35 sb.txt
137712 -rw-r--r--   1 denise   users     569855 Sep 29 12:55 smsup2.exe
137644 -rw-------   1 root     sys         161 Jul 11 12:18 softinittesoftcm
137706 -rw-r--r--   1 denise   users         39 Sep 29 12:48 srvpr.exe
137682 -rw-r--r--   1 denise   users         38 Aug 15 12:14 steve.h
137685 -rw-r--r--   1 denise   users      14675 Aug 30 15:08 target.exe
137711 -rw-r--r--   1 denise   users     229630 Sep 29 12:54 tcp41a.exe
137700 -rw-r--r--   1 denise   users    1954453 Sep 29 12:26 tnds2.exe
137703 -rw-r--r--   1 denise   users     364270 Sep 23 09:50 upgrade.exe
137663 -rwx-----x   1 denise   users         88 Aug  9 13:43 whoon
137678 -rw-r--r--   1 denise   users     191495 Aug 30 15:00 win95app.exe
```

The inode number contains: the location of files and directories on the disk; access permissions; owner and group ids; file link count; time of last modification; time of last access; device identification number for special files; and a variety of other information. inode numbers are used extensively by the system as you change directories and perform various work.

ls -p

Since you may have subdirectories within the directory you are listing, you may want to use the **-p** option to **ls,** which puts a "/" in after directory names as shown in the following example:

```
$ ls -p /home/denise

.Xauthority
.cshrc
.elm/
.exrc
.fmrc.orig
.glancerc
.gpmhp
.history
.login
.lrom/
.mailrc
.netscape-bookmarks.html
.netscape-cache/
.netscape-cookies
.netscape-history
.netscape-newsgroups-news.spry.com
.netscape-newsgroups-newsserv.hp.com
.netscape-preferences
.newsrc-news.spry.com
.newsrc-newsserv.hp.com
.profile
.rhosts
.sh_history
.softbuildrc
.softinit.orig
.sw/
.vue/
.vueprofile
.xinitrc
.xsession
27247b.exe
410pt1.exe
410pt2.exe
41ndir.exe
41nds1.exe
41nds4.exe
41nwad.exe
41rtr2.exe
HPDA1.EXE
Mail/
N3212B6.EXE
SCSI4S.EXE
clean
clean2
clean3
content.exe
dsenh.exe
eg1
eg2
en0316bz.exe
en0316tb.exe
explore.exe
flexi_cd.exe
fred.h
hal.c
hpd10117.exe
hpdlinst.txt
hpux.patches
j2577a.exe
ja95up.exe
msie10.exe
n32e12n.exe
nfs197.exe
pass.sb
plusdemo.exe
ps4x03.exe
psg
quik_res.exe
rclock.exe
rkhelp.exe
roni.mak
sb.txt
```

```
smsup2.exe
softinit.remotesoftcm
srvpr.exe
steve.h
target.exe
tcp41a.exe
tnds2.exe
upgrade.exe
whoon
win95app.exe
```

ls -R

Since the subdirectories you are listing probably have files and subdirectories beneath them, you may want to recursively list these. The **-R** option to **ls** shown in the following example will perform this recursive listing. This listing is very long because it includes the files and directories contained within directories under **/home/denise**:

```
$ ls -R /home/denise

.Xauthority
.cshrc
.elm
.exrc
.fmrc.orig
.glancerc
.gpmhp
.history
.login
.lrom
.mailrc
.netscape-bookmarks.html
.netscape-cache
.netscape-cookies
.netscape-history
.netscape-newsgroups-news.spry.com
.netscape-newsgroups-newsserv.hp.com
.netscape-preferences
.newsrc-news.spry.com
.newsrc-newsserv.hp.com
.profile
.rhosts
.sh_history
.softbuildrc
.softinit.orig
.sw
.vue
.vueprofile
.xinitrc
.xsession
27247b.exe
410pt1.exe
410pt2.exe
41ndir.exe
41nds1.exe
41nds4.exe
```

```
41nwad.exe
41rtr2.exe
HPDA1.EXE
Mail
N3212B6.EXE
SCSI4S.EXE
clean
clean2
clean3
content.exe
dsenh.exe
eg1
eg2
en0316bz.exe
en0316tb.exe
explore.exe
flexi_cd.exe
fred.h
hal.c
hpdl0117.exe
hpdlinst.txt
hpux.patches
j2577a.exe
ja95up.exe
msie10.exe
n32e12n.exe
nfs197.exe
pass.sb
plusdemo.exe
ps4x03.exe
psg
quik_res.exe
rclock.exe
rkhelp.exe
roni.mak
sb.txt
smsup2.exe
softinit.remotesoftcm
srvpr.exe
steve.h
target.exe
tcp41a.exe
tnds2.exe
upgrade.exe
whoon
win95app.exe

/home/denise/.elm:
last_read_mail

/home/denise/.lrom:
LRAAAa27637.CC
LRBAAa27637.CC
LROM.AB
LROM.AB.OLD
LROM.AB.1k1
LROM.SET

/home/denise/.netscape-cache:
cache306C05510015292.gif
cache306C05560025292.gif
cache306C05560035292.gif

/home/denise/.sw:
sessions

/home/denise/.sw/sessions:

/home/denise/.vue:
.trashinfo
Desktop
apps
palettes
sessions
startlog
```

```
    types

    /home/denise/.vue/Desktop:
    Five
    Four
    One
    Six
    Three
    Two

    /home/denise/.vue/Desktop/Five:

    /home/denise/.vue/Desktop/Four:

    /home/denise/.vue/Desktop/One:

    /home/denise/.vue/Desktop/Six:

    /home/denise/.vue/Desktop/Three:

    /home/denise/.vue/Desktop/Two:

    /home/denise/.vue/apps:
    GeneralTools
    NetworkTools

    /home/denise/.vue/apps/GeneralTools:
    Communication
    GeneralReadme
    Media
    Performance
    SoftBench
    System_Admin
    System_Info
    Unsupported
    Utilities
    X_Terminals

    /home/denise/.vue/apps/GeneralTools/Communication:
    Elm

    /home/denise/.vue/apps/GeneralTools/Media:
    Audio
    Capture
    Image

    /home/denise/.vue/apps/GeneralTools/Performance:
    Glance
    GlanceTerminal
    PcsExtract
    PcsUtility

    /home/denise/.vue/apps/GeneralTools/SoftBench:
    Browse
    Build
    CompareFiles
    CustomerService
    Debug
    Developer
    Dr_SoftBench
    Edit
    Mailer
    Monitor
    ShowFunctions
    ToolManager
    Training

    /home/denise/.vue/apps/GeneralTools/System_Admin:
    ChangePassword
    EditResources
    EditVuewmrc
    FontClientSrvr
    ReloadActions
    Sam
    SetNetworking
```

```
ShutdownSystem

/home/denise/.vue/apps/GeneralTools/System_Info:
BLINKLINK
C
C++_compiler
DDE
GlancePlus
GlancePlusPak
HPPAK
PcsInfo

/home/denise/.vue/apps/GeneralTools/Unsupported:
Clipboard
Columns
DisplayFont
Dr_Vue
FinancialCalc
ListVueTypes
ListWinInfo
ListWinProps
XserverInfo

/home/denise/.vue/apps/GeneralTools/Utilities:
Bitmap
CheckSpelling
CompareFiles
Compress
Console
CountWords
CreateAction
DigitalClock
DirSize
DiskSpaceAvail
Dtterm
ExecuteCmd
Hpterm
IconEditor
ListEnvVars
ListSymbols
Make
PrintFormat
PrintUnformat
PrinterInfo
RefreshScreen
ShredFile
StringSearch
SystemLoad
Tar
TarList
TarUnpack
TextEditor
TypeFile
Uncompress
Vi
WatchErrors
Xterm
XwdCapture
XwdDisplay

/home/denise/.vue/apps/GeneralTools/X_Terminals:
Local_Clients
Utilities

/home/denise/.vue/apps/GeneralTools/X_Terminals/Local_Clients:
HpxtHpterm
HpxtListClients
HpxtLogScreen
HpxtVt320
HpxtVt320Serial
HpxtXflash
HpxtXterm
HpxtXtermSerial

/home/denise/.vue/apps/GeneralTools/X_Terminals/Utilities:
```

```
HpxtAdmin
KeyMapper
SelectVUEwm

/home/denise/.vue/apps/NetworkTools:
NetworkReadme

/home/denise/.vue/palettes:

/home/denise/.vue/sessions:
current
current.font
current.huh
current.old
home

/home/denise/.vue/sessions/current:
vue.resources
vue.session
vue.settings

/home/denise/.vue/sessions/current.font:
C

/home/denise/.vue/sessions/current.font/C:
vue.font.h

/home/denise/.vue/sessions/current.huh:
vue.resources
vue.session
vue.settings

/home/denise/.vue/sessions/current.old:
vue.resources
vue.session
vue.settings

/home/denise/.vue/sessions/home:
vue.resources
vue.session
vue.settings

/home/denise/.vue/types:
tools

/home/denise/.vue/types/tools:
ChangePassword
CreateAction
DigitalClock
IconEditor
PersonalReadme
SystemLoad

/home/denise/Mail:
```

ls Summary

I have shown you what I believe to be the most important, and most
often used, **ls** options. Because you may have future needs to list files
and directories based on other criteria, I will provide you with a list of
most **ls** options. There is no substitute, however, for issuing the **man**

command. Whatever I provide is only a summary. Viewing the man pages for **ls** will give you much more information. The following is a summary of the more commonly used **ls** options:

ls - List the contents of a directory

Options

-a	List all entries.
-b	Print nongraphic characters.
-c	Use time file was last modified for producing order in which files are listed.
-d	List only the directory name, not its contents.
-f	Assume each argument is a directory.
-g	Only the group is printed and not the owner.
-i	Print the inode number in the first column of the report.
-m	List the contents across the screen separated by commas.
-n	Numbers for UID and GID are printed instead of names.
-o	List the information in long form (-l) except that group is omitted.
-p	Put a slash (/) at the end of directory names.
-q	Nonprinting characters are represented by a "?".
-r	Reverse the order in which files are printed.
-s	Show the size in blocks instead of bytes.
-t	List in order of time saved with most recent first.
-u	Use time of last access instead of last modification for determining order in which files are printed.
-x	List files in multicolumn format as shown in examples.
-A	Same as -a except current and parent directories aren't listed.
-C	Multicolumn output produced.
-F	Directory followed by a "/", executable by an "*", symbolic link by an "@", and FIFO by a "|".
-L	List file or directory to which link points.
-R	Recursively list subdirectories.
-1	Output will be listed in single column format.

There are also some shorthand command names for issuing **ls** with options. For instance, **ll** is equivalent to **ls -l** and **lsr** is equivalent to **ls -R**. We will also cover creating an "alias" whereby you can define your own shorthand for any command in an upcoming chapter.

You can selectively list and perform other file related commands with wild cards. The following section covers file name expansion and wild cards.

File Name Expansion and Wild Cards

Before we cover additional file system related commands, it is worth taking a look at file name expansion. An overview of file name expansion is useful to insure you're comfortable with this topic before we cover additional commands.

Table 4-2 lists some common file name expansion and pattern matching.

Table 4-2   File Name Expansion and Pattern Matching

Character(s)	Example	Description
*	1) **ls *.c**	Match zero or more characters
?	2) **ls conf.?**	Match any single character
[list]	3) **ls conf.[co]**	Match any character in list
[lower-upper]	4) **ls libdd.9873[5-6].sl**	Match any character in range
str{str1,str2,str3,...}	5) **ls ux*.{700,300}**	Expand str with contents of { }
~	6) **ls -a ~**	Home directory
~username	7) **ls -a ~gene**	Home directory of username

The following descriptions of the examples shown in Table 4-2 are more detailed.

1) To list all files in a directory that end in ".c", you could do the following:

```
$  ls *.c
        conf. SAM.c   conf.c
```

2) To find all of the files in a directory named "conf" with an extension of one character, you could do the following:

```
$  ls conf.?
        conf.c   conf.o   conf.1
```

3) To list all of the files in a directory named "conf" with only the extension "c" or "o", you could do the following:

```
$  ls conf.{co}
        conf.c   conf.o
```

4) To list files with similar names but a field that covers a range, you could do the following:

```
$  ls libdd9873[5-6].sl
        libdd98735.sl   libdd98736.sl
```

5) To list files that start with "ux", and have the extension "300" or "700", you could do the following:

```
$  ls ux*.{700,300}
        uxbootlf.700   uxinstfs.300   unistkern.300
        unistkern.700 unistlf.700
```

6) To list the files in your home directory you could use ~:

```
$  ls -a ~
       .               .cshrc.org  .login      .shrc.org
       ..              .exrc       .login.org  .vue
       .chsrc  .history            .profile    .vueprofile
```

7) To list the files in the home directory of a user you could do the following:

```
$  ls -a ~gene
       .               .history     .vue        splinedat
       ..              .login       .vueprofile trail.txt
       .chsrc          .login.org   ESP-File    under.des
       .cshrc.org      .profile     Mail        xtra.part
       .exrc           .shrc.org    opt
```

Chapter 5

File System Related Commands

pwd and cd

When we covered absolute and relative path names we used the **cd** command to change directory. You can be at any point in the file system hierarchy and use **cd** to change to the desired directory, provided you have the necessary permissions to change to that directory.

In one of the examples shown earlier we used an absolute pathname to change to a directory as shown in the following example:

```
$ cd /home/denise/.netscape-cache
```

Regardless of your current location in the file system hierarchy, this will change you to the directory **/home/denise/.netscape-cache**. If, however, your current location in the file system hierarchy is **/home/denise** then you could use a relative pathname to change to **.netscape-cache** as shown in the following example:

```
$ cd .netscape-cache
```

In order to change directory to a place in the file system relative to your current location, you need a way to determine your current location. The **pwd** command, for **p**rint **w**orking **d**irectory, can do this for you. Going back to the previous example in which we changed directories using the relative path, we could have first issued the **pwd** command to see that our location was **/home/denise** as shown in the following example:

```
$ pwd
/home/denise
$ cd .netscape-cache
$ pwd
$ /home/denise/.netscape-cache
$
```

pwd takes some of the mystery out of determining your current directory.

Let's now take a look at moving up a level in the directory tree using two dots:

```
$ pwd
/home/denise/.netscape-cache
$ cd ..
$ pwd
/home/denise
$
```

The two dot notation moves you to the parent directory of your current directory.

To return to your home directory you could issue the **cd** command with no arguments as shown in the following example:

```
$ pwd
/tmp
$ cd
$ pwd
/home/denise
$
```

This shows that no matter what your current location in the file system hierarchy, you can always get back quickly to your home directory. We won't get into shell parameters for some time, but there is a shell parameter which defines your *home* location as shown in the following example:

```
$ pwd
/tmp
$ cd $HOME
$ pwd
/home/denise
$
```

Using the **pwd** and **cd** commands you can always obtain your current directory and change to any directory.

cd - Change to a new current directory.

Arguments

none	Change to home directory. This is defined by the HOME environment variable
..	The two dot notation moves you to the parent directory of your current directory.
path	You can specify either an absolute or relative path to change to.

pwd - Print Working Directory so you know your current location.

Examples

```
$ pwd
/home/denise/.netscape-cache
$ cd ..
$ pwd
/home/denise
$
```

chmod

The chmod command is used to change the permissions on a file. Let's start our discussion of **chmod** with the listing of the file **sort** shown earlier:

```
$ ls -l sort
-rwxr-x--x   1 marty       users       120 Jul 26 10:20 sort
```

Figure 5-1 shows a breakdown of the permissions on **sort**.

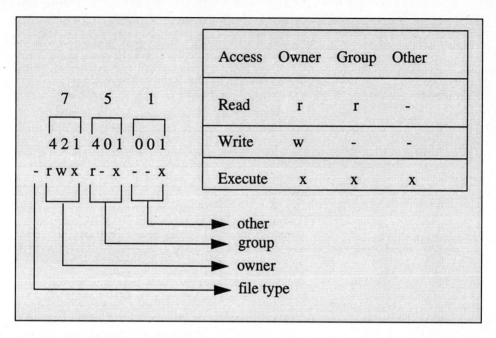

Figure 5-1   Permissions of File **sort**

You have very little control over the type of file defined. You do, however, have a great deal of control over the permissions of this file if it belongs to you. The **chmod** command is used to change the permissions on a file or directory. If you are the owner of the file you can have a field day changing the permissions on the file.

There are two means by which you can change the permissions: symbolic or numeric. I'll focus first on the numeric mode, since the numbers involved are easy to manage and I sometimes find new HP-UX users get hung up on the meaning of some of the symbols. I'll then cover the symbols and include the symbol meanings in the **chmod** summary. I decided to use the symbols in the summary because the numeric mode, which I much prefer, is becoming obsolete. The **chmod** manual page is strewn with references to "obsolescent form" whenever the numeric mode is covered.

First of all, what do I mean by numbers? Looking at the numbers for **sort** we see permissions of 751: 7 for *owner* (hundreds position), 5 for *group* (tens position), and 1 for *other* (ones position). Figure 5-2 helps with the meanings of the positions.

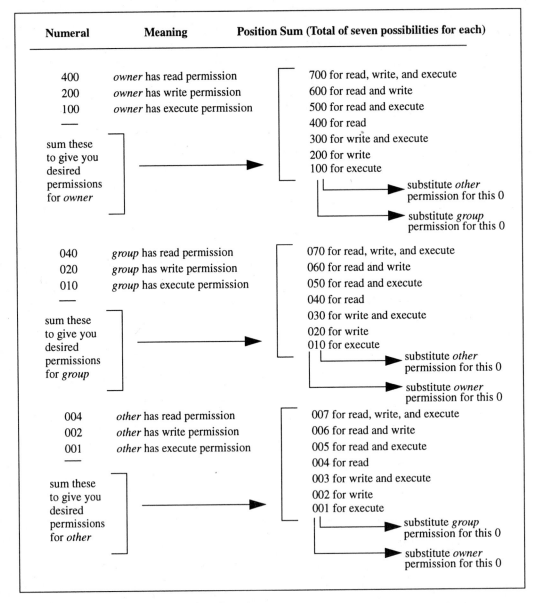

Figure 5-2   Numerical Permissions Summary

Selecting the desired permissions for *owner*, *group*, and *other*, you use the **chmod** command to assign those permissions to a file or directory. Some of these permission possibilities are infrequently used such as execute only, because you usually need to have read access to a file in order to execute it; however, I included all possibilities in figure 5-2 for completeness. In addition to the permission mode bits shown in figure 5-2, there are also miscellaneous mode bits which you don't need to be concerned with at this time.

If you decided that you would like to add write permission of the file **sort** for *group*, and remove all permissions for *other*, you would simply execute the **chmod** command with the appropriate numeric value. The following set of commands first list the existing permissions for **sort**, next change the permissions on **sort**, and finally list the new permissions on **sort**:

```
$ ls -l sort
-rwxr-x--x   1 marty        users        120 Jul 26 10:20 sort

$ chmod 770 sort

$ ls -l sort
-rwxrwx---   1 marty        users        120 Jul 26 10:20 sort
```

The same set of commands to change the permissions using the symbolic mode would be:

```
$ ls -l sort
-rwxr-x--x   1 marty        users        120 Jul 26 10:20 sort

$ chmod g+w,o-x sort

$ ls -l sort
-rwxrwx---   1 marty        users        120 Jul 26 10:20 sort
```

In symbolic mode you issue the **chmod** command and specify who will be affected by the change [user (u), group (g), other (o), or all (a)], the operation you wish to perform [add (+), delete (-), or replace (=)] permissions, and the permission you wish to specify [read (r), write (w), or execute (x)]. In the previous example using symbolic mode, write (w) permission is being added (+) for *group* (g), and execute (x) permission is being removed (-) for *other* (o).

The following is a summary of some of the more commonly used symbols of **chmod**:

chmod - Change permissions of specified files using the following symbolic mode list.

Symbol of who is affected:

u	User is affected.
g	Group is affected.
o	Other is affected.
a	All users are affected.

Operation to perform:

+	Add permission.
-	Remove permission.
=	Replace permission.

Permission specified:

r	Read permission.
w	Write permission.
x	Execute permission.
u	Copy user permissions.
g	Copy group permissions.
o	Copy other permissions.

cp

The **cp** command is used to copy a file from one location to another location. You do not alter the original file when you perform a copy. Provided you have access to the destination directory to which you wish to copy a file, you can place as many copies of a file in that destination as you wish. Permissions were covered in Chapter 4 if you need to go back and review that material.

The upcoming bullet list describes some of the types of copies you can perform with **cp**. Since there are many file types in HP-UX (as covered in Chapter 3), and many ways to specify path names for the source and destination files being copied, this list might help you understand the many ways **cp** can be used:

- Copy a source file to a new file name.

- Copy several source files to a different directory.

- Copy several source files to the same directory.

- Copy an entire directory to a different directory.

- Copy several directories to different directories.

The following is an example of copying a file to a new file name within the same directory:

```
$ cp krsort krsort.sav
```

What if the file **krsort.sav** already exists? The answer is it is replaced by the new **krsort.sav** being copied. To prevent such mishaps (officially called an overwrite) from occurring, you would use the **-i** option to **cp**. **-i** asks you if you wish to overwrite the file before the copy takes place. If your response is affirmative then the old file is over written with the new file.

The following example first shows a listing of the contents of a directory. Using the **cp** with the **-i** option, we copy the file **krsort.c** to **krsortorig.c**, a file which already exists. By responding *n* when asked if we want to over write **krsortorig.c,** the file is not overwritten and no copy takes place:

```
$ ll
total 168
-rwxr-xr-x    1 denise    users         34592 Oct 31 11:27 krsort
-rwxr-xr-x    1 denise    users          3234 Oct 31 11:27 krsort.c
-rwxr-xr-x    1 denise    users         32756 Oct 31 11:27 krsort.dos
-rw-r--r--    1 denise    users          9922 Oct 31 11:27 krsort.q
-rwxr-xr-x    1 denise    users          3085 Oct 31 11:27 krsortorig.c
$ cp -i krsort.c krsortorig.c
overwrite krsortorig.c? (y/n) n
$
```

cp - Copy files and directories.

Options

-i   Interactive copy whereby you are prompted to confirm you wish to overwrite an existing file.

-f   Force existing files to be overwritten by files being copied if there is a conflict in file names.

-p   Preserve permissions when copying.

-r   Copy recursively.

-R   Copy recursively except permissions are different.

mv

The **mv** command is used to move a file or directory from one location to another location. You can also move multiple files.

The following example shows a listing of a directory, the move of a file **krsort.c** to **krsort.test.c** within this directory, and a listing of the directory showing the file has been moved:

```
$ ls -l
total 168
-rwxr-xr-x   1 denise     users        34592 Oct 31 15:17 krsort
-rwxr-xr-x   1 denise     users         3234 Oct 31 15:17 krsort.c
-rwxr-xr-x   1 denise     users        32756 Oct 31 15:17 krsort.dos
-rw-r--r--   1 denise     users         9922 Oct 31 15:17 krsort.q
-rwxr-xr-x   1 denise     users         3085 Oct 31 15:17 krsortorig.c
$ mv krsort.c krsort.test.c
$ ls -l
total 168
-rwxr-xr-x   1 denise     users        34592 Oct 31 15:17 krsort
-rwxr-xr-x   1 denise     users        32756 Oct 31 15:17 krsort.dos
-rw-r--r--   1 denise     users         9922 Oct 31 15:17 krsort.q
-rwxr-xr-x   1 denise     users         3234 Oct 31 15:17 krsort.test.c
-rwxr-xr-x   1 denise     users         3085 Oct 31 15:17 krsortorig.c
$
```

What if the destination file already exists? You guessed it, HP-UX is more than happy to write over the destination file. Using the **-i** option, **mv** will ask you to confirm overwriting a file before it does so. The following example shows an attempt to move **krsort.test.c** to **krsortorig.c**. The user is alerted to the fact that **krsortorig.c** already exists and chooses not to let the move take place:

```
$ ls -l
total 168
-rwxr-xr-x   1 denise     users        34592 Oct 31 15:17 krsort
-rwxr-xr-x   1 denise     users        32756 Oct 31 15:17 krsort.dos
-rw-r--r--   1 denise     users         9922 Oct 31 15:17 krsort.q
-rwxr-xr-x   1 denise     users         3234 Oct 31 15:17 krsort.test.c
-rwxr-xr-x   1 denise     users         3085 Oct 31 15:17 krsortorig.c
$ mv -i krsort.test.c krsortorig.c
remove krsortorig.c? (y/n) n
$ ls -l
total 168
-rwxr-xr-x   1 denise     users        34592 Oct 31 15:17 krsort
```

```
-rwxr-xr-x   1 denise    users      32756 Oct 31 15:17 krsort.dos
-rw-r--r--   1 denise    users       9922 Oct 31 15:17 krsort.q
-rwxr-xr-x   1 denise    users       3234 Oct 31 15:17 krsort.test.c
-rwxr-xr-x   1 denise    users       3085 Oct 31 15:17 krsortorig.c
$
```

Because the response was not in the affirmative, the move does not take place and the original **krsortorig.c** remains intact.

mv - Copy files and directories.

Options

-i	Interactive copy whereby you are prompted to confirm you wish to overwrite an existing file.
-f	Force existing files to be overwritten by files being copied if there is a conflict in file names.
-p	Preserve permissions when copying.

mkdir

How nice it would be to have a command to make a directory any time you wish. You could then use this command to create directories and thereby organize your files in multiple directories in a way similar to organizing files in a filing cabinet. The **mkdir** command allows you to do just that - make a directory.

This is an incredibly simple command. You specify the name of the directory to create. In the following example we'll look at the contents of a directory with the **ls** command, use **mkdir** to make the directory named **default.permissions**, and then perform another **ls** to see the new directory:

```
$ ls -l
total 2
drwxr-xr-x   2 denise   users        1024 Oct 31 11:27 krsort.dir.old
$ mkdir default.permissions
$ ls -l
total 4
drwxr-xr-x   2 denise   users        1024 Oct 31 11:27 krsort.dir.old
drwxr-xr-x   2 denise   users          24 Oct 31 11:32 default.permissions
$
```

The new directory has been produced with default permissions for the user *denise. group* and *other* have both read and execute permissions for this directory.

What if you wanted to create a directory with specific permissions on it instead of default permissions? You could use the **-m** option to **mkdir** and specify the mode or permissions you want. To give all users read permission on the **krsort.dir.new** directory you would issue the following:

```
$ mkdir -m "a=r" read.permissions
$ ls -l
total 6
drwxr-xr-x   2 denise   users        1024 Oct 31 11:27 krsort.dir.old
drwxr-xr-x   2 denise   users          24 Oct 31 11:32 default.permissions
dr--r--r--   2 denise   users          24 Oct 31 11:33 read.permissions
$
```

Remember the symbolic versus numeric mode of permissions? This **mkdir** command shows the symbolic mode, which although I do not like it as much as the numeric mode, should be used because the numeric mode is becoming obsolete.

You don't have to stop at creating a directory with only one level of depth. You can create a new directory with any number of subdirectories in it with the **-p** option. Intermediate directories are created with the **-p** option. Let's now create a directory named **level1**, with the directory **level2** beneath it, and the directory **level3** below **level2** in the following

example. The **ls** command with the **-R** option will recursively list the
directories below **level1**:

```
$ mkdir -p level1/level2/level3
$ ls -R level1
level2

level1/level2:
level3

level1/level2/level3:
$
```

After creating the directory **level1** and issuing the **ls** command, we
can see that **level2** is indeed beneath **level1**, and **level3** is beneath **level2**.

mkdir - Create specified directories.

Options

    -m   Specify the mode (permissions) of the directory.

    -p   Create intermediate directories to achieve the full path. If
            you want to create several layers of directory down you
            would use **-p**.

rm

The **rm** command removes one or more files from a directory and can
also be used to remove the directory itself. Going back to our earlier discussion on permissions, you must have both *write* and *execute* permissions on a directory in order to remove a file from it. If you own the
directory from which you are going to remove files, then it is likely you
can remove files from it. If, however, you don't have the appropriate permissions on a directory, then the **rm** of files will fail.

As with some of the other commands we have covered, you can use
the **-i** option, which asks you to confirm each file as it is removed. This
means if you are asked if you really wish to remove a file and you

respond *n* then the file will not be removed. If you respond *y* the file will be removed.

You can also use the **-r** (or **-R**) option to recursively delete the contents of directories and then delete the directories. This means you can recursively delete the files and directories specified. If there is any question in your mind about whether or not you wish to recursively delete files and directories, then use the **-i** option along with **-r**.

You can use the *-f* option to remove files and directories, which will perform removes <u>without</u> asking you to confirm them.

The following example performs a long listing of the directory **krsort.dir.new**, interactively prompts the user to see if he or she wants to delete the files in this directory, and then lists the contents of this directory again showing all files have <u>not</u> been deleted because the user responded *n*:

```
$ ls -l krsort.dir.new
total 168
-rwxr-xr-x  1 denise    users      34592 Oct 27 18:44 krsort
-rwxr-xr-x  1 denise    users       3234 Oct 27 18:46 krsort.c
-rwxr-xr-x  1 denise    users      32756 Oct 27 18:46 krsort.dos
-rw-r--r--  1 denise    users       9922 Oct 27 18:46 krsort.q
-rwxr-xr-x  1 denise    users       3085 Oct 27 18:46 krsortorig.c
$ rm -i krsort.dir.new/*
../krsort.dir.new/krsort: ? (y/n) n
../krsort.dir.new/krsort.c: ? (y/n) n
../krsort.dir.new/krsort.dos: ? (y/n) n
../krsort.dir.new/krsort.q: ? (y/n) n
../krsort.dir.new/krsortorig.c: ? (y/n) n
$ ls -l krsort.dir.new
total 168
-rwxr-xr-x  1 denise    users      34592 Oct 27 18:44 krsort
-rwxr-xr-x  1 denise    users       3234 Oct 27 18:46 krsort.c
-rwxr-xr-x  1 denise    users      32756 Oct 27 18:46 krsort.dos
-rw-r--r--  1 denise    users       9922 Oct 27 18:46 krsort.q
-rwxr-xr-x  1 denise    users       3085 Oct 27 18:46 krsortorig.c
$
```

Note that the response to being asked if the file should be deleted was *n* in all cases. This means that none of the files has been removed. A *y* response to any question would result in that file being removed from the directory. To interactively delete a directory you would combine the options **-i** and **-r** of the **rm** command. If, however, you do not delete every file in a directory, then the directory will not be removed if the **-i** option is used. The first part of the following example shows all but the file **krsort** being removed from the directory **krsort.dir.new**. The directory will not be deleted because this file still exists. When the file is removed in the second part of this example, the directory itself is then deleted:

```
$ rm -ir krsort.dir.new
directory krsort.dir.new: ? (y/n) y
krsort.dir.new/krsort: ? (y/n) n
krsort.dir.new/krsort.c: ? (y/n) y
krsort.dir.new/krsort.dos: ? (y/n) y
krsort.dir.new/krsort.q: ? (y/n) y
krsort.dir.new/krsortorig.c: ? (y/n) y
krsort.dir.new: ? (y/n) y
rm: directory krsort.dir.new not removed.  Directory not empty

$ rm -ir krsort.dir.new
directory krsort.dir.new: ? (y/n) y
krsort.dir.new/krsort: ? (y/n) y
krsort.dir.new: ? (y/n) y
$
```

rm - Remove files and directories.

Options

-i   Interactive remove whereby you are prompted to confirm you wish to remove an existing file.

-f   Force files to be removed.

-r (-R)   Recursively remove the contents of the directory and then the directory itself.

rmdir

The **rmdir** command removes one or more directories. The directory must be empty in order to be removed. You can also specify more than one directory to be removed. Going back to our earlier discussion on permissions, you must have both *write* and *execute* permissions on the parent of a directory to be removed in order to remove it.

As with some of the other commands we have covered, you can use the **-i** option which asks you to confirm each directory as it is removed. This means if you are asked if you really wish to remove a directory and you respond *n* then it will not be removed. If you respond *y* it will be removed.

The order in which you specify directories are to be removed is significant. If you want to remove both a directory and its subdirectory, you must specify the subdirectory to be removed first. If you specify the parent directory rather than its subdirectory to be removed first, the remove of the parent directory will fail because it is not empty.

You can use the **-f** option to force removal of directories, which will perform removes <u>without</u> asking you to confirm them.

The following example performs a long listing of the directory **krsort.dir.new** showing that this directory has in it a file called **.dotfile**. When we attempt to remove this directory with **rmdir,** a message is displayed informing us this directory is not empty. The file **.dotfile** in this directory will prevent the **rmdir** command from removing **krsort.dir.new**. After removing **.dotfile,** we are able to remove the directory with **rmdir**.

```
$ ls -al ../krsort.dir.new
total 4
drwxr-xr-x    2 denise    users         1024 Oct 27 18:57 .
drwxrwxr-x    4 denise    users         1024 Oct 27 18:40 ..
-rw-r--r--    1 denise    users            0 Oct 27 18:56 .dotfile
$ rmdir -i ../krsort.dir.new
../krsort.dir.new: ? (y/n) y
rmdir: ../krsort.dir.new: Directory not empty
$ rm ../krsort.dir.new/.dotfile
$ rmdir -i ../krsort.dir.new
../krsort.dir.new: ? (y/n) y
$
```

rmdir has now successfully removed **krsort.dir.new** with **.dotfile** gone:

rmdir - Remove directories.

Options

-i	Interactive remove whereby you are prompted to confirm you wish to remove a directory
-f	Force directories to be removed.
-p	If, after removing a directory, the parent directory is empty then remove it also. This goes on until a parent directory is encountered that is not empty.

Using Commands

Using the cd, pwd, ls, mkdir, and cp commands

Now that we have covered some of these commands in an "isolated" fashion, let's put some of the commands together.

Let's start by viewing the hierarchy of a directory under *denise's* home directory called **krsort.dir.old,** as shown in Figure 5-3:

```
$ cd /home/denise/krsort.dir.old
$ pwd
/home/denise/krsort.dir.old
$ ls -l
total 168
-rwxr-xr-x   1 denise     users        34592 Oct 27 18:20 krsort
-rwxr-xr-x   1 denise     users         3234 Oct 27 17:30 krsort.c
-rwxr-xr-x   1 denise     users        32756 Oct 27 17:30 krsort.dos
-rw-r--r--   1 denise     users         9922 Oct 27 17:30 krsort.q
-rwxr-xr-x   1 denise     users         3085 Oct 27 17:30 krsortorig.c
$
```

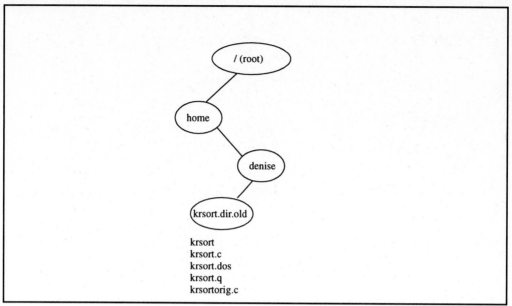

Figure 5-3   /home/denise/krsort.dir.old

We can then make a new directory called **krsort.dir.new** and copy a file to it, as shown in Figure 5-4:

```
$ mkdir ../krsort.dir.new
$ cp krsort ../krsort.dir.new
$ ls -l ../krsort.dir.new
total 68
-rwxr-xr-x   1 denise   users        34592 Oct 27 18:27 krsort
$
```

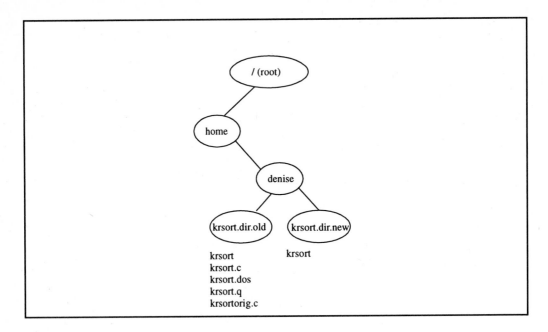

Figure 5-4   /home/denise/krsort.dir.new

Now let's try the **-i** option to **cp**. If we attempt to copy a file to an existing file name we'll be asked if we wish to overwrite the destination file. We are alerted to the fact that the destination file already exists and we can then select a new name for the file we wish to copy, as shown in Figure 5-5:

```
$ pwd
/users/denise/krsort.dir.old
$ cp -i krsort ../krsort.dir.new
overwrite ../krsort.dir.new/krsort? (y/n) n
$ cp krsort ../krsort.dir.new/krsort.new.name
$ ls -l ../krsort.dir.new
total 136
-rwxr-xr-x    1 denise   users      34592 Oct 27 18:27 krsort
-rwxr-xr-x    1 denise   users      34592 Oct 27 18:29 krsort.new.name
$
```

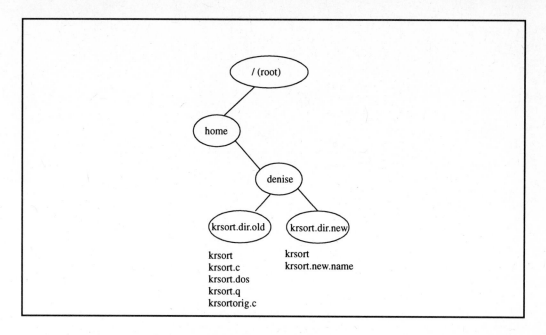

Figure 5-5 **/home/denise/krsort.dir.new/krsort.new.name** Added

We can also use a wildcard with **cp** to copy all files in **krsort.dir.old** to **krsort.dir.new,** as shown in Figure 5-6:

```
$ cp * ../krsort.dir.new
$ ls -l ../krsort.dir.new
total 236
-rwxr-xr-x   1 denise   users      34592 Oct 27 18:30 krsort
-rwxr-xr-x   1 denise   users       3234 Oct 27 18:30 krsort.c
-rwxr-xr-x   1 denise   users      32756 Oct 27 18:30 krsort.dos
-rwxr-xr-x   1 denise   users      34592 Oct 27 18:29 krsort.new.name
-rw-r--r--   1 denise   users       9922 Oct 27 18:30 krsort.q
-rwxr-xr-x   1 denise   users       3085 Oct 27 18:30 krsortorig.c
$
```

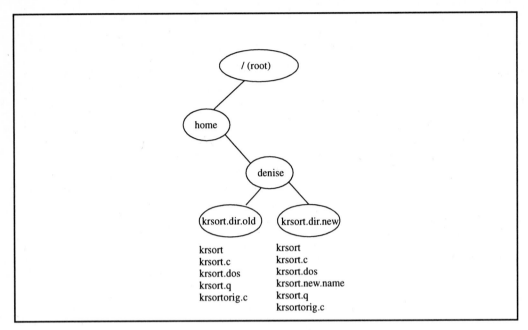

Figure 5-6   All Files Copied to **/home/denise/krsort.dir.new**

Using the mv Command

Let's start over at the point where the **krsort.dir.new** directory is empty, as shown in Figure 5-7:

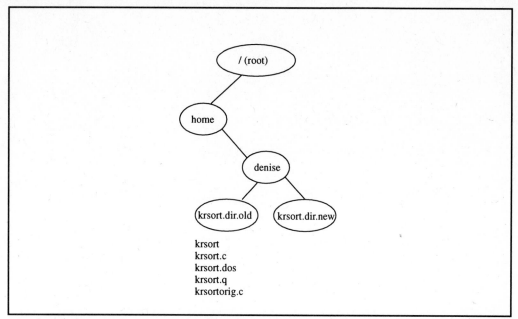

Figure 5-7   Empty **/home/denise/krsort.dir.new** Directory

    We can now move the file **krsort** to the **krsort.dir.new** directory, as shown in Figure 5-8:

```
$ mv krsort ../krsort.dir.new
$ ls -l ../krsort.dir.new
total 68
-rwxr-xr-x   1 denise    users        34592 Oct 27 18:20 krsort
$
```

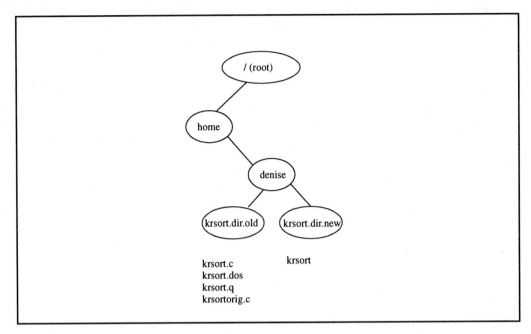

Figure 5-8   krsort Moved to **/krsort.dir.new**

If we now attempt to move **krsort** to the **krsort.dir.new** directory with the **-i** option and write over the file **krsort** we get the following:

```
$ mv -i krsort ../krsort.dir.new/krsort
remove ../krsort.dir.new/krsort? (y/n) n
$
```

Because we used the **-i** option to **mv** we are asked if we wish to allow a file to be overwritten with the move. Because we responded *n* to the question, the file will not be overwritten.

We can also use a wildcard with the **mv** command to copy all files from the **krsort.dir.old** directory to the **krsort.dir.new** directory. Without the **-i** option, any files in the **krsort.dir.new** directory are overwritten by files that have the same name, as shown in Figure 5-9:

```
$ mv * ../krsort.dir.new
$ ls -l ../krsort.dir.new
```

```
 total 168
-rwxr-xr-x    1 denise    users       34592 Oct 27 18:44 krsort
-rwxr-xr-x    1 denise    users        3234 Oct 27 18:46 krsort.c
-rwxr-xr-x    1 denise    users       32756 Oct 27 18:46 krsort.dos
-rw-r--r--    1 denise    users        9922 Oct 27 18:46 krsort.q
-rwxr-xr-x    1 denise    users        3085 Oct 27 18:46 krsortorig.c
$
```

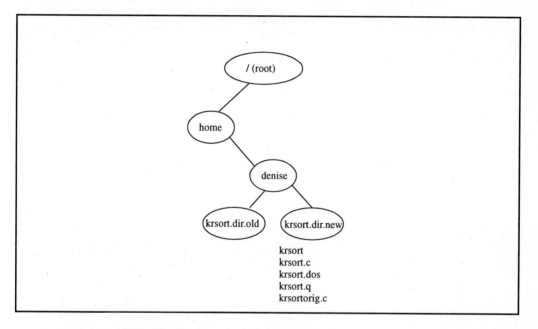

Figure 5-9   All Files Moved to **/home/denise/krsort.dir.new**

Down and Dirty with the rm and rmdir Commands

The most feared command in the UNIX world, with good reason I might add, is the **rm** command. **rm** will remove whatever you want whenever you want with no questions asked unless you use the **-i** option.

Want to blow away your system instantly? **rm** would be more than happy to help you. As an average user, and not the system administrator, it is unlikely you have the permissions to do so. It is, however, unnerving to know that this is a possibility. In addition, it is likely that you have permissions remove all of your own files and directories. All of this can be easily avoided by simply using the **-i** option to **rm**.

Let's assume that **krsort.dir.new** and **krsort.dir.old** are identical directories, as shown in Figure 5-10:

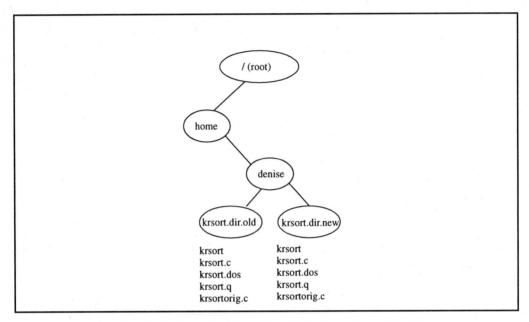

Figure 5-10   **/home/denise/krsort.dir.old** and **/home/denise/krsort.dir.new** Identical

To interactively remove files from **krsort.dir.new** you would do the following:

```
$ rm -i ../krsort.dir.new/*
../krsort.dir.new/krsort: ? (y/n) n
../krsort.dir.new/krsort.c: ? (y/n) n
../krsort.dir.new/krsort.dos: ? (y/n) n
../krsort.dir.new/krsort.q: ? (y/n) n
../krsort.dir.new/krsortorig.c: ? (y/n) n
$ ls -l ../krsort.dir.new
total 168
-rwxr-xr-x   1 denise    users        34592 Oct 27 18:44 krsort
-rwxr-xr-x   1 denise    users         3234 Oct 27 18:46 krsort.c
-rwxr-xr-x   1 denise    users        32756 Oct 27 18:46 krsort.dos
-rw-r--r--   1 denise    users         9922 Oct 27 18:46 krsort.q
-rwxr-xr-x   1 denise    users         3085 Oct 27 18:46 krsortorig.c
$
```

This obviously resulted in nothing being removed from **krsort.dir.new** because we responded *n* when asked if we wanted to delete files.

Let's now go ahead and add a file beginning with a "." to **krsort.dir.new**. The **touch** command does just that, touches a file to create it with no contents, as shown in Figure 5-11:

```
$ touch ../krsort.dir.new/.dotfile
$ ls -al ../krsort.dir.new
total 172
drwxr-xr-x    2 denise    users         1024 Oct 27 18:54 .
drwxrwxr-x    4 denise    users         1024 Oct 27 18:40 ..
-rw-r--r--    1 denise    users            0 Oct 27 18:56 .dotfile
-rwxr-xr-x    1 denise    users        34592 Oct 27 18:44 krsort
-rwxr-xr-x    1 denise    users         3234 Oct 27 18:46 krsort.c
-rwxr-xr-x    1 denise    users        32756 Oct 27 18:46 krsort.dos
-rw-r--r--    1 denise    users         9922 Oct 27 18:46 krsort.q
-rwxr-xr-x    1 denise    users         3085 Oct 27 18:46 krsortorig.c
$
```

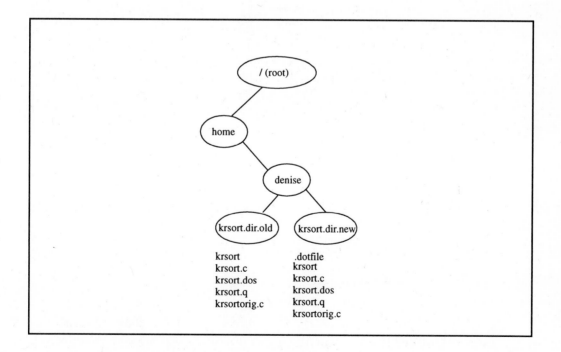

Figure 5-11 **/home/denise/krsort.dir.new** with **.dotfile**

If we now attempt to remove files using the same **rm** command earlier issued we'll see the following, as shown in Figure 5-12:

```
$ rm -i ../krsort.dir.new/*
../krsort.dir.new/krsort: ? (y/n) y
../krsort.dir.new/krsort.c: ? (y/n) y
../krsort.dir.new/krsort.dos: ? (y/n) y
../krsort.dir.new/krsort.q: ? (y/n) y
../krsort.dir.new/krsortorig.c: ? (y/n) y
$ ls -al ../krsort.dir.new
total 4
drwxr-xr-x    2 denise    users          1024 Oct 27 18:57 .
drwxrwxr-x    4 denise    users          1024 Oct 27 18:40 ..
-rw-r--r--    1 denise    users             0 Oct 27 18:56 .dotfile
```

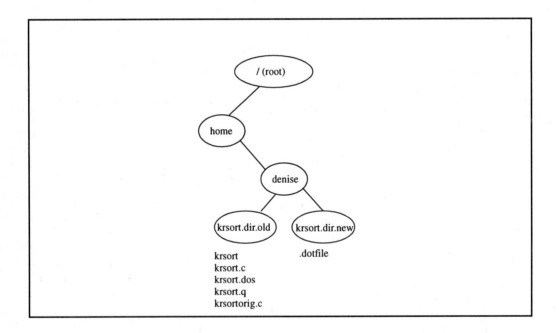

Figure 5-12   Only .dotfile Left in /home/denise/krsort.dir.new

The "*" used as a wildcard with the **rm** command does not remove the file **.dotfile**. The file **.dotfile** in this directory will prevent the **rmdir** command from removing **krsort.dir.new**. This file must first be removed before the **rmdir** command can successfully delete **krsort.dir.new.**

```
$ rmdir -i ../krsort.dir.new
../krsort.dir.new: ? (y/n) y
rmdir: ../krsort.dir.new: Directory not empty
$ rm ../krsort.dir.new/.dotfile
$ rmdir -i ../krsort.dir.new
../krsort.dir.new: ? (y/n) y
$
```

rmdir has now successfully removed **krsort.dir.new** with **.dotfile** gone, as shown in Figure 5-13:

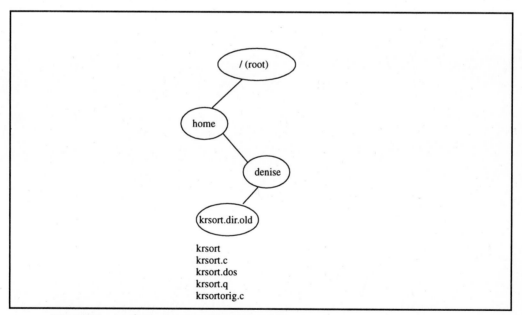

Figure 5-13 **rmdir** Removes **/home/denise/krsort.dir.new**

Chapter 6

HP-UX Tools

Redirection

Before we cover commands, let's talk about redirection for a minute. I'll cover redirection under shell programming, but for now I want to give you just a quick introduction to redirection so we can more effectively cover some of the commands in this chapter. Figure 6-1 shows some of the most common forms of redirection.

Figure 6-1   Commonly Used Redirection Forms

Command	Example	Description
I	**ll I grep .login**	Perform a long listing and search for the text **.login**
<	**wc -l < .login**	Standard input redirection: execute **wc** (word count) and list number of lines (**-l**) in **.login**
>	**ps -ef > /tmp/processes**	Standard output redirection: execute **ps** and send output to file **/tmp/processes**

Command	Example	Description
>>	ps -ef >> /tmp/processes	Append standard output: execute **ps** and append output to the end of file **/tmp/processes**
>!	ps -ef >! /tmp/processes	Append output redirection and override **noclobber**: write over **/tmp/processes** even if it exists
>>!	ps -ef >>! /tmp/processes	Append standard output and override **noclobber**: append to the end of **/tmp/processes**

When you issue a command, such as those we have been using throughout this book, the result of the command is displayed on the screen. In the UNIX world we call this *standard output*. Similarly, your keyboard is usually *standard input*. Using the symbols shown in Figure 6-1 you can redirect from standard input and standard output. For instance, rather than display the output on the screen you can send the output to file. We will use some of these redirection forms in upcoming examples.

Viewing Files with cat, more, pg, head, and tail

To begin with, let's look at a long file. In fact, let's look at a file so long that it will not fit on your screen if you were to print out the contents of the file to your screen.

The **cat** command (short for concatenate) does just this, prints out the file to your screen. If, however, the file is long, then you will only see the end of the file on your screen. Remember the user **denise** from earlier in the book? She had a lot of files in her directory. Let's list the files in her directory and redirect the output to a file called **listing** with the following command:

```
$ ls -a /home/denise > listing
```

When we **cat listing** to the screen we will see only the end of it as shown in Figure 6-2. We know this is the end of the file because I have issued **cat** with the **-n** option that includes line numbers. The line numbers indicate this is not the beginning of the file.

```
                                 cat −n example
     106   rclock.exe
     107   rkhelp.exe
     108   sb.txt
     109   shellupd.exe
     110   smsup2.exe
     111   softinit.remotesoftcm
     112   srvpr.exe
     113   tabnd1.exe
     114   target.exe
     115   tcp41a.exe
     116   tnds2.exe
     117   trace.TRC1
     118   trace.TRC1.Z.uue
     119   upgrade.exe
     120   uue.syntax
     121   v103.txt
     122   whoon
     123   win95app.exe
     124   wsdrv1.exe
     125   wsos21.exe
     126   wsos22.exe
     127   wsos23.exe
     128   xferp110.zip
$
```

Figure 6-2   cat -n Command

Seeing only the end of this file is not what we had in mind. Using the **pg** (for page) we will see one screen at time, as shown in Figure 6-3:

```
┌─────────────────────────────────────────────────────────────────────────┐
│ ▭                              pg example                            ▫ □ │
├─────────────────────────────────────────────────────────────────────────┤
│ .                                                                         │
│ ..                                                                        │
│ .CbtOptSet                                                                │
│ .Xauthority                                                               │
│ .cshrc                                                                    │
│ .cshrc.orig                                                               │
│ .elm                                                                      │
│ .exrc                                                                     │
│ .fmrc                                                                     │
│ .fmrc.orig                                                                │
│ .glancerc                                                                 │
│ .gpmhp                                                                    │
│ .history                                                                  │
│ .login                                                                    │
│ .lrom                                                                     │
│ .mailrc                                                                   │
│ .netscape-bookmarks.html                                                  │
│ .netscape-cache                                                           │
│ .netscape-history                                                         │
│ .netscape-newsgroups-news.spry.com                                        │
│ .netscape-newsgroups-newsserv.hp.com                                      │
│ .netscape-preferences                                                     │
│ .newsrc-news.spry.com                                                     │
│ :█                                                                        │
└─────────────────────────────────────────────────────────────────────────┘
```

Figure 6-3   pg Command

The **more** command produces the same output as **pg,** as shown in Figure 6-4.

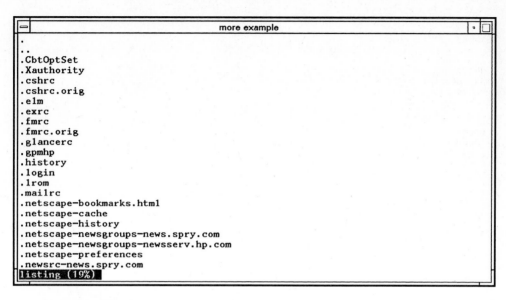

Figure 6-4   more Command

This is more like it; now we can scroll on a screen by screen basis with both **pg** and **more**. It is, however, sometimes desirable to view only the beginning or end of a file. You can use the **head** command to view the beginning of a file and the **tail** command to view the bottom of a file. The following two examples of **head** and **tail** (see Figures 6-5 and 6-6) show viewing the first 20 lines of **listing** and the last 20 lines of **listing** respectively.

```
┌─────────────────────────────────────────────────────────────────────────┐
│ ▭                              head example                           ▫ □ │
├─────────────────────────────────────────────────────────────────────────┤
│ $ head -20 listing                                                        │
│ .                                                                         │
│ ..                                                                        │
│ .CbtOptSet                                                                │
│ .Xauthority                                                               │
│ .cshrc                                                                    │
│ .cshrc.orig                                                               │
│ .elm                                                                      │
│ .exrc                                                                     │
│ .fmrc                                                                     │
│ .fmrc.orig                                                                │
│ .glancerc                                                                 │
│ .gpmhp                                                                    │
│ .history                                                                  │
│ .login                                                                    │
│ .lrom                                                                     │
│ .mailrc                                                                   │
│ .netscape-bookmarks.html                                                  │
│ .netscape-cache                                                           │
│ .netscape-history                                                         │
│ .netscape-newsgroups-news.spry.com                                        │
│ $ █                                                                       │
│                                                                           │
└─────────────────────────────────────────────────────────────────────────┘
```

Figure 6-5   head Command

```
┌─────────────────────────────────────────────────────────────────────────┐
│ ▭                              tail example                           ▫ □ │
├─────────────────────────────────────────────────────────────────────────┤
│ $ tail -20 listing                                                        │
│ shellupd.exe                                                              │
│ smsup2.exe                                                                │
│ softinit.remotesoftcm                                                     │
│ srvpr.exe                                                                 │
│ tabnd1.exe                                                                │
│ target.exe                                                                │
│ tcp41a.exe                                                                │
│ tnds2.exe                                                                 │
│ trace.TRC1                                                                │
│ trace.TRC1.Z.uue                                                          │
│ upgrade.exe                                                               │
│ uue.syntax                                                                │
│ v103.txt                                                                  │
│ whoon                                                                     │
│ win95app.exe                                                              │
│ wsdrv1.exe                                                                │
│ wsos21.exe                                                                │
│ wsos22.exe                                                                │
│ wsos23.exe                                                                │
│ xferp110.zip                                                              │
│ $ █                                                                       │
│                                                                           │
└─────────────────────────────────────────────────────────────────────────┘
```

Figure 6-6   tail Command

The command you use depends on the information you wish to display. My personal preference, whether viewing the contents of a large file or a long listing of files, is to use **more**. I don't have a good reason for this and all I can say is that we are creatures of habit and I have always used **more**. The following are command summaries for **cat**, **pg**, **more**, **head**, and **tail**. I included some of the most frequently used options associated with these commands. Since none of the commands are difficult to use I suggest you try each command and see if one suits your needs better than the others.

Here are summaries of the **cat, pg, more, head,** and **tail** commands.

cat - Display, combine, append, copy, or create files.

Options

-	Used as a substitute for specifying a file name when you want to use the keyboard for standard input.
-n	Line numbers are displayed along with output lines.
-p	Replace multiple consecutive empty lines with only one empty line.
-s	This is silent mode which suppresses information about nonexistent files.
-u	Output is unbuffered which means it is handled character by character.
-v	Print most nonprinting characters visibly.

pg - Display all or parts of a file.

Options

-number	The number of lines you wish to display.
-p string	Use string to specify a prompt.
-c	Clear the screen before displaying the next page of the file.

-f	Don't split lines being displayed.
-n	A command is issued as soon as a command letter is typed rather than having to issue a new line character.

more - Display all or parts of a file on screen at a time.

Options

-c	Clear the screen before displaying the next page of the file.
-d	Display a prompt at the bottom of the screen with brief instructions.
-f	Wrap text to fit screen and judge page length accordingly.
-n	The number of lines in the display window is set to n.
-s	Squeeze multiple consecutive empty lines into one empty line.

head - Provide only the first few lines of a file.

Options

-c	The output is produced with a specified number of bytes.
-l	The output is produced with a specified number of lines. This is the default.
-n count	The number of bytes or lines is specified by count. You can also use -count to specify the number of bytes or lines, which is shown in the example. The default count is 10.

tail - Provide the last few lines of a file.

Options

-bnumber   Specify number of blocks from end of file you wish to begin displaying.

-cnumber   Specify number of characters from end of file you wish to begin displaying.

-nnumber   Specify number of lines from end of file you wish to begin displaying. You can also specify a number or minus sign and number, as shown in the example, to specify the number of lines from the end of file to begin displaying.

split

Some files are just too long. The file **listing** we earlier looked at may be more easily managed if split into multiple files. We can use the **split** command to make **listing** into files 25 lines long as shown in Figure 6-7.

```
                                    split example                          
$ ll listing
-rw-------   1 denise    users        1430 Dec 19 16:30 listing
$
$ split -l 25 listing
$
$ ll x*
-rw-------   1 denise    users         330 Dec 19 16:40 xaa
-rw-------   1 denise    users         267 Dec 19 16:40 xab
-rw-------   1 denise    users         268 Dec 19 16:40 xac
-rw-------   1 denise    users         256 Dec 19 16:40 xad
-rw-------   1 denise    users         274 Dec 19 16:40 xae
-rw-------   1 denise    users          35 Dec 19 16:40 xaf
$ 
```

Figure 6-7   split Command

Note that the split command produced several files from **listing** called **xaa**, **xab**, and so on. The **-l** option is used to specify the number of lines in files produced by **split**.

Here is a summary of the **split** command.

split - Split a file into multiple files.

Options

               -l line_count   Split the file into files with line_count lines per file.

               -b n   Split the file into files with n bytes per file.

wc

We know that we have split **listing** into separate files of 25 lines each, but how many lines were in **listing** originally? How about the number of words in **listing**? Those of us who get paid by the word for some of the articles we write often want to know this. How about the number of characters in a file? The **wc** command can produce a word, line, and character count for you. Figure 6-8 shows issuing the **wc** command with the **-wlc** options, which produces a count of words with the **-w** option, lines with the **-l** option, and characters with the **-c** option.

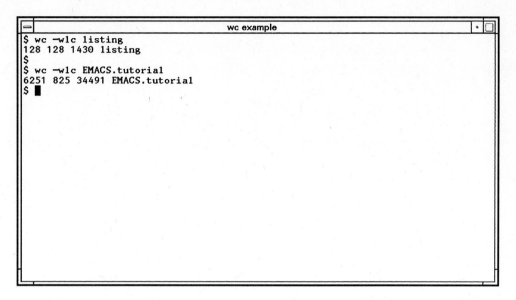

```
⊟                                         wc example                                    □ □
$ wc -wlc listing
128 128 1430 listing
$
$ wc -wlc EMACS.tutorial
6251 825 34491 EMACS.tutorial
$ ■
```

Figure 6-8   wc Command

Notice that the number of words and lines produced by **wc** is the same for the file **listing**. This is because each line contains exactly one word. When we display the words, lines, and characters with the **wc** command for the text file **EMACS.tutorial** we can see that the number of words is 6251, the number of lines is 825, and the number of characters is 34491. In a text file, in this case a tutorial, you would expect there to be many more words than lines.

Here is a summary of the **wc** command.

wc - Produce a count of words, lines, and characters.

Options

-l   Print the number of lines in a file.

-w   Print the number of words in a file.

-c   Print the number of characters in a file.

grep

Here in the information age we have too much information. We are constantly trying to extract the information we are after from stacks of information. The **grep** command is used to search for text and display it. Figure 6-9 shows creating a long listing for **/home/denise** and using **grep** we search for patterns.

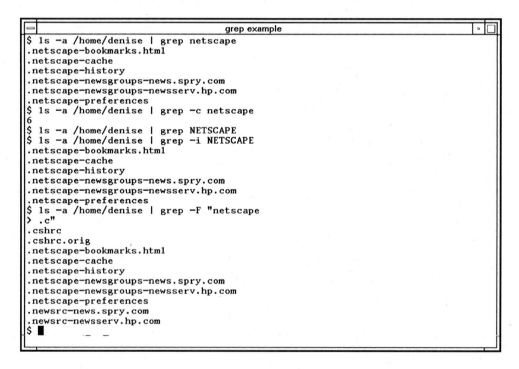

```
                            grep example
$ ls -a /home/denise | grep netscape
.netscape-bookmarks.html
.netscape-cache
.netscape-history
.netscape-newsgroups-news.spry.com
.netscape-newsgroups-newsserv.hp.com
.netscape-preferences
$ ls -a /home/denise | grep -c netscape
6
$ ls -a /home/denise | grep NETSCAPE
$ ls -a /home/denise | grep -i NETSCAPE
.netscape-bookmarks.html
.netscape-cache
.netscape-history
.netscape-newsgroups-news.spry.com
.netscape-newsgroups-newsserv.hp.com
.netscape-preferences
$ ls -a /home/denise | grep -F "netscape
> .c"
.cshrc
.cshrc.orig
.netscape-bookmarks.html
.netscape-cache
.netscape-history
.netscape-newsgroups-news.spry.com
.netscape-newsgroups-newsserv.hp.com
.netscape-preferences
.newsrc-news.spry.com
.newsrc-newsserv.hp.com
$
```

Figure 6-9   **grep** Command

First, we search for the pattern **netscape**. This produces a list of files, all of which begin with *.netscape*.

Next we use the **-c** option to create a count for the number of times that *netscape* is found. The result is 6.

Do you think **grep** is case sensitive? The next example shows searching for the pattern *NETSCAPE* and there are no matching patterns.

Using the **-i** option causes **grep** to ignore upper case and lower case and just search for the pattern, and again all of the original matches are found.

More than one pattern can be searched for also. Using the **-F** option both *netscape* and *.c* are searched for and a longer list of matches are found. Notice that two patterns to search for are enclosed in double quotes and are separated by a new line.

Here is a summary of the **grep** command.

grep - Search for text and display results.

Options

-c	Return the number of matches without showing you the text.
-h	Show the text with no reference to file names.
-i	Ignore the case when searching.
-l	Return the names of files containing a match without showing you the text.
-n	Return the line number of the text searched for in a file as well as the text itself.
-v	Return the lines that do not match the text you searched for.
-E	Search for more than one expression (same as **egrep**).
-F	Search for more than one expression (same as **fgrep**).

sort

Sometimes the contents of files are not sorted in the way you would like. You can use the **sort** command to sort files with a variety of options.

You may find as you use your HP-UX system more and more that your system administrator is riding you about the amount of disk space you are consuming. You can monitor the amount of disk space you are consuming with the **du** command. Figure 6-10 shows creating a file called **disk_space** that lists the amount of disk space consumed by files and directories and shows the first 20 lines of the file.

```
                                    sort example #1                              ▫ ▫
$ du -s * > disk_space
$
$ head -20 disk_space
1216      27247b.exe
240       410pt1.exe
288       410pt2.exe
74        41mac1.exe
368       41ndir.exe
736       41nds1.exe
1056      41nds4.exe
3056      41nwad.exe
1696      41rtr2.exe
68        EMACS.tutorial
2         Mail
3520      N3212B6.EXE
368       PHNE_6014
752       PHNE_6121
976       PHNE_6121.depot
20        PHNE_6121.text
2         Passwd
28        SCSI4S.EXE
36        aplay.exe
4         archives
$ ▪
```

Figure 6-10   sort Command Example #1

Notice that the result is sorted alphabetically. In many cases this is what you want. If the file were not sorted alphabetically you could use the **sort** command to do so. In this case we don't care as much about seeing entries in alphabetical order as we do in numeric order, that is, which files and directories are consuming the most space. Figure 6-11 shows sorting the file **disk_space** numerically with the **-n** option and reversing the order of the sort with the **-r** option so the biggest numbers appear first. We then specify the output file name with the **-o** option.

```
┌──────────────────────────── sort example #2 ──────────────────────────┐
│ $ sort -n -r disk_space -o disk_space_numeric                          │
│ $                                                                      │
│ $ head -20 disk_space_numeric                                          │
│ 288238   main.directory                                                │
│ 60336    emacs-19.28.tar                                               │
│ 8128     c3295n_a.exe                                                  │
│ 5024     trace.TRC1                                                    │
│ 4496     rkhelp.exe                                                    │
│ 3840     tnds2.exe                                                     │
│ 3520     n32e12n.exe                                                   │
│ 3520     N3212B6.EXE                                                   │
│ 3056     41nwad.exe                                                    │
│ 2784     nsh220e2.zip                                                  │
│ 2768     nsh220e3.zip                                                  │
│ 2752     nfs197.exe                                                    │
│ 2688     mbox                                                          │
│ 2160     msie10.exe                                                    │
│ 2032     nsh220e1.zip                                                  │
│ 2000     trace.TRC1.Z.uue                                              │
│ 1984     plusdemo.exe                                                  │
│ 1840     ja95up.exe                                                    │
│ 1776     hpd10117.exe                                                  │
│ 1712     wsos22.exe                                                    │
│ $ ■                                                                    │
└────────────────────────────────────────────────────────────────────────┘
```

Figure 6-11   **sort** Command Example #2

The following is a summary of the **sort** command.

sort - Sort lines of files (alphabetically by default).

Options

-b	Ignore leading spaces and tabs.
-c	Check if files are already sorted and if so do nothing.
-d	Ignore punctuation and sort in dictionary order

-f	Ignore the case of entries when sorting.
-i	Ignore non-ASCII characters when sorting.
-m	Merge sorted files.
-n	Sort in numeric order.
-o file	Specify the output file name rather than write to standard output.
-r	Reverse order of the sort by starting with the last letter of the alphabet or with the largest number as we did in the example.
+n	Skip n fields or columns before sorting.

cmp and diff

It is a fact of life that as you go about editing files you may occasionally lose track of what changes you have made to which files. You may then need to make comparisons of files. Let's take a look at two such commands, **cmp** and **diff**, and see how they compare files.

Let's assume we have modified a script called **llsum** (we'll study this script in a later chapter on shell programming). The unmodified version of **llsum** was saved as **llsum.orig**. Using the **head** command we can view the first 20 lines of **llsum** and then the first 20 lines of **llsum.orig**:

```
# head -20 llsum
#
#!/bin/sh
# Displays a truncated long listing (ll) and
# displays size statistics
# of the files in the listing.

ll $* | \
awk ' BEGIN { x=i=0; printf "%-25s%-10s%8s%8s\n",\
                     "FILENAME","OWNER","SIZE","TYPE" }
        $1 ~ /^[-dlps]/  {# line format for normal files
               printf "%-25s%-10s%8d",$9,$3,$5
               x = x + $5
                  i++
```

```
                          }
           $1 ~ /^-/ { printf "%8s\n","file" }  # standard file types
            $1 ~ /^d/ { printf "%8s\n","dir" }
            $1 ~ /^l/ { printf "%8s\n","link" }
            $1 ~ /^p/ { printf "%8s\n","pipe" }
            $1 ~ /^s/ { printf "%8s\n","socket" }
            $1 ~ /^[bc]/ { # line format for device files
                    printf "%-25s%-10s%8s%8s\n",$10,$3,"","dev"
                          }
#
# head -20 llsum.orig
#
#!/bin/sh
# Displays a truncated long listing (ll) and
# displays size statistics
# of the files in the listing.

ll $* | \
awk ' BEGIN { x=i=0; printf "%-16s%-10s%8s%8s\n",\
                        "FILENAME","OWNER","SIZE","TYPE" }
        $1 ~ /^[-dlps]/  {# line format for normal files
               printf "%-16s%-10s%8d",$9,$3,$5
               x = x + $5
                 i++
                          }
          $1 ~ /^-/ { printf "%8s\n","file" }  # standard file types
            $1 ~ /^d/ { printf "%8s\n","dir" }
            $1 ~ /^l/ { printf "%8s\n","link" }
            $1 ~ /^p/ { printf "%8s\n","pipe" }
            $1 ~ /^s/ { printf "%8s\n","socket" }
            $1 ~ /^[bc]/ { # line format for device files
                    printf "%-16s%-10s%8s%8s\n",$10,$3,"","dev"
                          }
```

I'm not sure what changes I made to **llsum.orig** to improve it, so we can first use **cmp** to see if indeed there are differences between the files.

```
$
$ cmp llsum llsum.orig
llsum llsum.orig differ: char 154, line 6
$
```

cmp does not report back much information, only that character 154 in the file at line 6 is different in the two files. There may indeed be other differences, but this is all we know about so far.

To get information about all of the differences in the two files we could use the **-l** option to **cmp**:

```
$ cmp -l llsum llsum.orig
  154  62  61
  155  65  66
  306  62  61
  307  65  66
  675  62  61
  676  65  66
```

This is not all that useful an output to me. I want to see not only the position of the differences, but the differences themselves.

Now we can use **diff** to describe all of the differences in the two files:

```
$ diff llsum llsum.orig
6c6
< awk ' BEGIN { x=i=0; printf "%-25s%-10s%8s%8s\n",\
---
> awk ' BEGIN { x=i=0; printf "%-16s%-10s%8s%8s\n",\
9c9
<            printf "%-25s%-10s%8d",$9,$3,$5
---
>            printf "%-16s%-10s%8d",$9,$3,$5
19c19
<            printf "%-25s%-10s%8s%8s\n",$10,$3,"","dev"
---
>            printf "%-16s%-10s%8s%8s\n",$10,$3,"","dev"
$
```

We now know that lines 6, 9, and 25 are different in the two files and these lines are also listed for us. From this we can see that the number 16 in **llsum.orig** was changed to 25 in the newer **llsum** file and this accounts for all of the differences in the two files. The less than sign (<) precedes lines from the first file, in this case **llsum**. The greater than sign (>) precedes lines from the second file, in this case **llsum.orig**. I made this change, going from starting the second group of information from character 16 to character 25, because I wanted the second group of information, produced by **llsum,** to start at column 25. The second group of information is the *owner* as shown in the following example.

```
$ llsum
FILENAME                      OWNER           SIZE     TYPE

README                        denise           810     file
backup_files                  denise          3408     file
biography                     denise           427     file
cshtest                       denise          1024      dir
gkill                         denise          1855     file
gkill.out                     denise           191     file
hostck                        denise           924     file
ifstat                        denise          1422     file
ifstat.int                    denise          2147     file
ifstat.out                    denise           723     file
introdos                      denise         54018     file
introux                       denise         52476     file
letter                        denise         23552     file
letter.auto                   denise         69632     file
letter.auto.recover           denise         71680     file
letter.backup                 denise         23552     file
letter.lck                    denise            57     file
letter.recover                denise         69632     file
llsum                         denise          1267     file
llsum.orig                    denise          1267     file
llsum.out                     denise          1657     file
llsum.tomd.out                denise          1356     file
psg                           denise           670     file
psg.int                       denise           802     file
psg.out                       denise           122     file
sam_adduser                   denise          1010     file
tdolan                        denise          1024      dir
trash                         denise          4554     file
trash.out                     denise           329     file
typescript                    denise          2017     file

The files listed occupy 393605 bytes (0.3754 Mbytes)
Average file size is 13120 bytes

$
```

When we run **llsum.orig** it is clear that the second group of information, which is the *owner*, starts at column 16 and not column 32:

```
$ llsum.orig
FILENAME        OWNER       SIZE    TYPE

README          denise       810    file
```

```
backup_files       denise        3408       file
biography          denise         427       file
cshtest            denise        1024        dir
gkill              denise        1855       file
gkill.out          denise         191       file
hostck             denise         924       file
ifstat             denise        1422       file
ifstat.int         denise        2147       file
ifstat.out         denise         723       file
introdos           denise       54018       file
introux            denise       52476       file
letter             denise       23552       file
letter.auto        denise       69632       file
letter.auto.recoverdenise        71680        file
letter.backup      denise       23552       file
letter.lck         denise          57       file
letter.recover     denise       69632       file
llsum              denise        1267       file
llsum.orig         denise        1267       file
llsum.out          denise        1657       file
llsum.tomd.out     denise        1356       file
psg                denise         670       file
psg.int            denise         802       file
psg.out            denise         122       file
sam_adduser        denise        1010       file
tdolan             denise        1024        dir
trash              denise        4554       file
trash.out          denise         329       file
typescript         denise        3894       file

The files listed occupy 395482 bytes (0.3772 Mbytes)
Average file size is 13182 bytes


script done on Mon Dec 11 12:59:18 1995

$
```

Here is a summary of the **cmp** and **diff** commands.

cmp - Compare the contents of two files. The byte position and line number of the first difference between the two files is returned.

Options

-l   Display the byte position and differing characters for all differences within a file.

-s   Work silently, that is only exit codes are returned.

diff - Compares two files and reports differing lines.

Options

-b	Ignore blanks at the end of a line.
-i	Ignore case differences.
-t	Expand tabs in output to spaces.
-w	Ignore spaces and tabs.

dircmp

Why stop at comparing files? You will probably have many directories in your user area as well. **dircmp** compares two directories and produces information about the contents of directories.

To begin with let's perform a long listing of two directories:

```
$ ll krsort.dir.old
total 168
-rwxr-xr-x   1 denise    users       34592 Oct 31 11:27 krsort
-rwxr-xr-x   1 denise    users        3234 Oct 31 11:27 krsort.c
-rwxr-xr-x   1 denise    users       32756 Oct 31 11:27 krsort.dos
-rw-r--r--   1 denise    users        9922 Oct 31 11:27 krsort.q
-rwxr-xr-x   1 denise    users        3085 Oct 31 11:27 krsortorig.c
$
$ ll krsort.dir.new
total 168
-rwxr-xr-x   1 denise    users       34592 Oct 31 15:17 krsort
-rwxr-xr-x   1 denise    users       32756 Oct 31 15:17 krsort.dos
-rw-r--r--   1 denise    users        9922 Oct 31 15:17 krsort.q
-rwxr-xr-x   1 denise    users        3234 Oct 31 15:17 krsort.test.c
-rwxr-xr-x   1 denise    users        3085 Oct 31 15:17 krsortorig.c
$
```

From this listing it is clear that there is one file unique to each directory. **krsort.c** appears in only the **krsort.dir.old** directory and **krsort.test.c** appears in only the **krsort.dir.new** directory. Let's now use **dircmp** to inform us of the differences in these two directories:

```
$ dircmp krsort.dir.old krsort.dir.new

krsort.dir.old only and krsort.dir.new only Page 1

./krsort.c            ./krsort.test.c




Comparison of krsort.dir.old krsort.dir.new Page 1

directory        .
same             ./krsort
same             ./krsort.dos
same             ./krsort.q
same             ./krsortorig.c

$
```

This is a useful output. First, the files that appear in only one directory are listed. Then, the files common to both directories are listed.

The following is a summary of the **dircmp** command.

dircmp - Compare directories.

Options

      -d   Compare the contents of files with the same name in both directories and produce a report of what must be done to make the files identical.

      -s   Suppress information about different files.

cut

There are times when you have an output that has too many fields in it. When we issued the **llsum** command earlier it produced four fields; FILENAME, OWNER, SIZE, and TYPE. What if we wanted to take this output and look at just the FILENAME and SIZE. We could modify the **llsum** script or we could use the **cut** command to eliminate the OWNER and TYPE fields with the following commands:

```
$ llsum | cut -c 1-25,37-43

FILENAME                 SIZE
README                    810
backup_files             3408
biography                 427
cshtest                  1024
gkill                    1855
gkill.out                 191
hostck                    924
ifstat                   1422
ifstat.int               2147
ifstat.out                723
introdos                54018
introux                 52476
letter                  23552
letter.auto             69632
letter.auto.recover     71680
letter.backup           23552
letter.lck                 57
letter.recover          69632
llsum                    1267
llsum.orig               1267
llsum.out                1657
llsum.tomd.out           1356
psg                       670
psg.int                   802
psg.out                   122
```

```
sam_adduser                          1010
tdolan                               1024
trash                                4554
trash.out                             329
typescript                             74

The files listed occupy 3 (0.373
Average file size is 1305
$
```

This has produced a list from **llsum** which is piped to **cut**. Only characters 1 through 25 and 37 through 43 have been extracted. These characters correspond to the fields we want. At the end of the output are two lines which are only partially printed. We don't want these lines, so we can use **grep -v** to eliminate them and print all other lines. The output of this command is saved to the file **llsum.out** at the end of this output, which we'll use later.

```
$ ./llsum | grep -v "bytes" | cut -c 1-25,37-43

FILENAME                 SIZE
README                    810
backup_files             3408
biography                 427
cshtest                  1024
gkill                    1855
gkill.out                 191
hostck                    924
ifstat                   1422
ifstat.int               2147
ifstat.out                723
introdos                54018
introux                 52476
letter                  23552
letter.auto             69632
letter.auto.recover     71680
letter.backup           23552
letter.lck                 57
letter.recover          69632
llsum                    1267
llsum.orig               1267
llsum.out                1657
llsum.tomd.out           1356
psg                       670
psg.int                   802
psg.out                   122
sam_adduser              1010
tdolan                   1024
trash                    4554
trash.out                 329
```

```
typescript                    1242
$ llsum | grep -v "bytes" | cut -c 1-25,37-4_3 > llsum.out
$
```

The following is a summary of the **cut** command with some of the more commonly used options.

cut - Extract specified fields from each line.

Options

-c list   Extract based on character position as shown in the example.

-f list   Extract based on fields.

-d char   The character following d is the delimiter when using the -f option. The delimiter is the character which separates fields.

paste

Files can be merged together in a variety of ways. If you want to merge files on a line by line basis you can use the **paste** command. The first line in the second file is pasted to the end of the first line in the first file and so on.

Let's use the **cut** command just covered and extract only the permissions field, or characters 1 through 10, to get only the permissions for files. We'll then save this in the file **ll.out**:

```
$ ll | cut -c 1-10

total 798
drwxrwxrwx
drwxrwxrwx
-rwxrwxrwx
-rwxrwxrwx
-rwxrwxrwx
drwxr-xr-x
-rwxrwxrwx
-rw-r--r--
-rwxrwxrwx
-rwxrwxrwx
-rwxr-xr-x
-rw-r--r--
-rw-r--r--
-rwxrwxrwx
-rw-r--r--
-rw-r--r--
-rw-r--r--
-rw-r--r--
-rw-rw-rw-
-rw-r--r--
-rw-r--r--
-rwxrwxrwx
-rwxr-xr-x
-rw-r--r--
-rw-r--r--
-rwxrwxrwx
-rwxr-xr-x
-rw-r--r--
-rwxrwxrwx
drwxr-xr-x
-rwxrwxrwx
-rw-r--r--
-rw-r--r--

$ ll -a | cut -c 1-10 > ll.out
$
```

We can now use the **paste** command to paste the permissions saved in the **ll.out** file to the other file-related information in the **llsum.out** file:

```
$ paste llsum.out ll.out

FILENAME                      SIZE        total 792
README                         810        -rwxrwxrwx
backup_files                  3408        -rwxrwxrwx
biography                      427        -rwxrwxrwx
cshtest                       1024        drwxr-xr-x
gkill                         1855        -rwxrwxrwx
gkill.out                      191        -rw-r--r--
hostck                         924        -rwxrwxrwx
ifstat                        1422        -rwxrwxrwx
ifstat.int                    2147        -rwxr-xr-x
```

```
        ifstat.out            723        -rw-r--r--
        introdos            54018        -rw-r--r--
        introux             52476        -rwxrwxrwx
        letter              23552        -rw-r--r--
        letter.auto         69632        -rw-r--r--
        letter.auto.recover 71680        -rw-r--r--
        letter.backup       23552        -rw-r--r--
        letter.lck             57        -rw-rw-rw-
        letter.recover      69632        -rw-r--r--
        ll.out               1057        -rw-r--r--
        llsum                1267        -rwxrwxrwx
        llsum.orig           1267        -rwxr-xr-x
        llsum.out            1657        -rw-r--r--
        llsum.tomd.out       1356        -rw-r--r--
        psg                   670        -rwxrwxrwx
        psg.int               802        -rwxr-xr-x
        psg.out               122        -rw-r--r--
        sam_adduser          1010        -rwxrwxrwx
        tdolan               1024        drwxr-xr-x
        trash                4554        -rwxrwxrwx
        trash.out             329        -rw-r--r--
        typescript            679        -rw-r--r--

        $
```

This has produced a list that includes *FILENAME* and *SIZE* from **llsum.out** and permissions from **ll.out**.

If both of the files have the same first field you can use the join command to merge the two files:

paste - Merge lines of files.

Options

    -d list   Use list as the delimiter between columns. You can use special escape sequences for list such as \n for newline and \t for tab.

join - Combine two presorted files that have a common key field.

Options

-a n   Produce the normal output and also generate a line for each line that can't be joined in 1 or 2.

-e string Replace empty fields in output with string.

-t char   Use char as the field separator.

tr

tr translates characters. **tr** is ideal for such tasks as changing case. For instance, what if you wanted to translate all lower case characters to upper case? The following example shows listing files that have the suffix "zip" and then translates these files into upper case:

```
$ ls -al *.zip
file1.zip
file2.zip
file3.zip
file4.zip
file5.zip
file6.zip
file7.zip
$ ls -al *.zip | tr "[:lower:]" "[:upper:]"
FILE1.ZIP
FILE2.ZIP
FILE3.ZIP
FILE4.ZIP
FILE5.ZIP
FILE6.ZIP
FILE7.ZIP
$
```

We use brackets in this case because we are translating a class of characters.

tr - Translate characters.

Options

       -A   Translate on a byte by byte basis.

       -d   Delete all occurrences of characters specified.

      [:class:] Translate from one character class to another such as from lower case class to upper case class as shown in the example.

Chapter 7

HP-UX Networking

Networking Background - Ethernet, IEEE 802.3, and TCP/IP

In order to understand how the networking on your HP-UX system works, you first need to understand the components of your network that exist on your HP-UX system. There are seven layers of network functionality that exist on your HP-UX system, as shown in Figure 7-1. I'll cover the bottom four layers at a cursory level, so you can see how each plays a part in the operation of your network. I'll spend most of the space covering the top layers, where you as a user will be issuing commands.

Layer Number	Layer Name	Data Form	Comments
7	Application		User applications.
6	Presentation		Applications prepared.
5	Session		Applications prepared.

Layer Number	Layer Name	Data Form	Comments
4	Transport	Packet	Port to port transportation handled by TCP
3	Network	Datagram	Internet Protocol (IP) handles routing by either going directly to the destination or default router.
2	Link	Frame	Data encapsulated in Ethernet or IEEE 802.3 with source and destination addresses.
1	Physical		Physical connection between systems. Usually thinnet or twisted pair.

Figure 7-1   ISO/OSI Network Layer Functions

I'll start reviewing Figure 7-1 at the bottom with layer 1 and describe each of the four bottom layers. This is the International Standards Organization Open Systems Interconnection (ISO/OSI) model. It is helpful to visualize the way in which networking layers interact.

Physical Layer

The beginning is the physical interconnect between the systems on your network. Without the **physical layer** you can't communicate between systems and all of the great functionality you would like to use will not be possible. The physical layer converts the data you would like to transmit to the analog signals that travel along the wire. I'll assume for now that whatever physical layer you have in place uses wires. With wireless communications and other developments taking place we won't be connecting systems with wires indefinitely. The information traveling into a network interface is taken off the wire and prepared for use by the next layer.

Link Layer

In order to connect to other systems local to your system, you use the link layer, which is able to establish a connection to all the other systems on your local segment. This is the layer where you have either IEEE 802.3 or Ethernet. Your HP-UX system supports both of these "encapsulation" methods. This is called encapsulation because your data is put in one of these two forms (either IEEE 802.3 or Ethernet). Data is transferred at the link layer in frames (just another name for data) with the source and destination addresses and some other information attached. You might think that because there are two different encapsulation methods that they must be different. This, however, is not the case. IEEE 802.3 and Ethernet are nearly identical. This is the reason your HP-UX system can handle both types of encapsulation. So, with the bottom two layers you have a physical connection between your systems and data that is encapsulated into one of two formats with a source and destination address attached. Figure 7-2 lists the components of an Ethernet encapsulation and includes comments about IEEE 802.3 encapsulation where appropriate.

destination address	6 bytes	address data is sent to
source address	6 bytes	address data is sent from
type	two bytes	this is the "length count" in 802.3
data	46-1500 bytes	38-1492 bytes for 802.3, the difference in these two data sizes (MTU) can be seen with the **ifconfig** command
crc	4 bytes	checksum to detect errors

Figure 7-2   Ethernet Encapsulation

One interesting item is the difference in the maximum data size between IEEE 802.3 and Ethernet of 1492 and 1500 bytes, respectively. This is the Maximum Transfer Unit (MTU). The data in Ethernet is called a *frame* (the re-encapsulation of data at the next layer up is called a *datagram* in IP, and encapsulation at two levels up is called a *packet* for TCP).

Keep in mind that Ethernet and IEEE 802.3 will run on the same physical connection, but there are indeed differences between the two encapsulation methods.

Network Layer

Next we work up to the third layer, which is the network layer. This layer on UNIX systems is synonymous with Internet Protocol (IP). Data at this layer is called *datagrams*. This is the layer that handles the routing of data around the network. Data that gets routed with IP sometimes encounters an error of some type, which is reported back to the source system with an Internet Control Message Protocol (ICMP) message.

Unfortunately, the information IP uses does not conveniently fit inside an Ethernet frame, so you end up with fragmented data. This is really re-encapsulation of the data, so you end up with a lot of inefficiency as you work your way up the layers.

IP handles routing in a simple fashion. If data is sent to a destination connected directly to your system, then the data is sent directly to that system. If, on the other hand, the destination is not connected directly to your system, the data is sent to the default router. The default router then has the responsibility to handle getting the data to its destination.

Transport Layer

This layer can be viewed as one level up from the network layer because it communicates with *ports*. TCP is the most common protocol found at this level and it forms packets which are sent from port to port. These ports are used by network programs such as **telnet**, **rlogin**, **ftp**, and so on. You can see that these programs, associated with ports, are the highest level we have covered while analyzing the layer diagram.

Internet Protocol (IP) Addressing

The Internet Protocol address (IP address) is either a class "A," "B," or "C" address (there are also class "D" and "E" addresses I will not cover). A class "A" network supports many more nodes per network than either a class "B" or "C" network. IP addresses consist of four fields. The purpose of breaking down the IP address into four fields is to define a node (or host) address and a network address. Figure 7-3 summarizes the relationships between the classes and addresses.

Address Class	Networks	Nodes per Network	Bits Defining Network	Bits Defining Nodes per Network
A	a few	the most	8 bits	24 bits
B	many	many	16 bits	16 bits
C	the most	a few	24 bits	8 bits
Reserved	-	-	-	-

Figure 7-3   Comparison of Internet Protocol (IP) Addresses

These bit patterns are significant in that the number of bits defines the ranges of networks and nodes in each class. For instance, a class A address uses 8 bits to define networks and a class C address uses 24 bits to define networks. A class A address therefore supports fewer networks than a class C address. A class A address, however, supports many more nodes per network than a class C address. Taking these relationships one step further, we can now view the specific parameters associated with these address classes in Figure 7-4.

Figure 7-4   Address Classes

Address Class	Networks Supported	Nodes per Network	Address Range		
A	127	16777215	0.0.0.1	-	127.255.255.254
B	16383	65535	128.0.0.1	-	191.255.255.254
C	2097157	255	192.0.0.1	-	223.255.254.254
Reserved	-	-	224.0.0.0	-	255.255.255.255

Looking at the 32-bit address in binary form, you can see how to determine the class of an address:

Class "A"

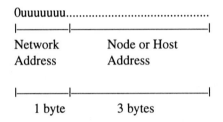

net.host.host.host

A class "A" address has the first bit set to 0. You can see how so many nodes per network can be supported with all of the bits devoted to the node or host address. The first bit of a class A address is 0 and the remaining 7 bits of the network portion are used to define the network. There are then a total of 3 bytes devoted to defining the nodes with a network.

Figure 7-4 Address Classes (Continued)

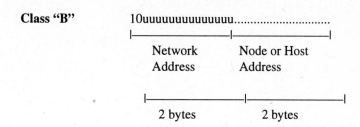

Class "B"

```
                10uuuuuuuuuuuuuuu..............................
                |—————————————————|————————————————|
                    Network            Node or Host
                    Address            Address

                |—————————————————|————————————————|
                    2 bytes            2 bytes
```

net.net.host.host

A class "B" address has the first bit set to a 1 and the second bit to a 0. There are more networks supported here than with a class A address, but fewer nodes per network. With a class B address there are 2 bytes devoted to the network portion of the address and 2 bytes devoted to the node portion of the address.

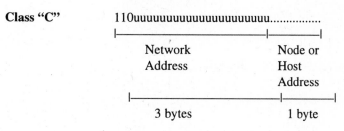

Class "C"

```
                110uuuuuuuuuuuuuuuuuuuuuuu................
                |————————————————————————————|—————————|
                    Network                      Node or
                    Address                      Host
                                                 Address
                |————————————————————————————|—————————|
                    3 bytes                      1 byte
```

net.net.net.host

A class "C" address has the first bit and second bit set to 1 and the third bit is 0. The greatest number of networks and fewest number of nodes per network are associated with a class C address. With a class C address there are 3 bytes devoted to the network and 1 byte devoted to the nodes within a network.

Every interface on your network must have a unique IP address. Systems that have two network interfaces must have two unique IP addresses.

Let's now switch to the high level and look at using some common networking commands on HP-UX.

Using Networking

The ISO/OSI model is helpful for visualizing the way in which the networking layers interact. The model does not, however, tell you how to use the networking. This is really your goal. For all of the examples the local host is **system1** and the remote host is **system2** as shown in Figure 7-5.

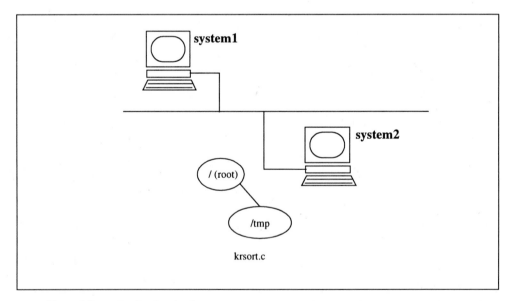

Figure 7-5   system1 and system2

ARPA Services (Communication among Systems with Different OS)

APRA services is a means by which any two systems can communicate. They do not have to be running the same operating system. This means that ARPA supports its own set of commands with which you should familiarize yourself. The following sections summarize these commands.

File Transfer Protocol (ftp)   Transfer files, or multiple files, from one system to another. This is often used when transferring files between an HP-UX workstation and a personal computer or VAX, etc. The following example shows copying the file **/tmp/krsort.c** from system2 (remote host) to the local directory on system1 (local host).

	comments
$ ftp system2	Issue ftp command
Connected to system2.	
system2 FTP server (Version 16.2) ready.	
Name (system2:root): root	Login to system2
Password required for root.	
Password:	Enter password
User root logged in.	
Remote system type is UNIX.	
Using binary mode to transfer files.	
ftp> **cd /tmp**	**cd** to **/tmp** on system2
CWD command successful	
ftp> **get krsort.c**	Get **krsort.c** file
PORT command successful	
Opening BINARY mode data connection for **krsort.c**	
Transfer complete.	

	comments
2896 bytes received in 0.08 seconds	
ftp> **bye**	Exit ftp
Goodbye.	
$	

In this example both systems are running HP-UX; however, the commands you issue through **ftp** are operating system independent. The **cd** for change directory and **get** commands used above work for any operating system on which **ftp** is running. If you become familiar with just a few **ftp** commands, you may find that transferring information in a heterogeneous networking environment is not difficult.

Chances are that you will be using your HP-UX system(s) in a heterogenous environment and may therefore use **ftp** to copy files and directories from one system to another. Since **ftp** is so widely used, I'll describe some of the more commonly used **ftp** commands.

ftp - File Transfer Program for copying files across a network.

The following list includes some commonly used **ftp** commands. This list is not complete.

           ascii   User is affected. Set the type of file transferred to ASCII. This means you will be transferring an ASCII file from one system to another. This is the default so you don't have to set it.

                    Example: **ascii**

binary   Set the type of file transferred to binary. This means you'll be transferring a binary file from one system to another. If, for instance, you want to have a directory on your HP-UX system which will hold applications that you will copy to non-HP-UX systems, then you will want to use binary transfer.

Example: **binary**

cd   Change to the specified directory on the remote host.

Example: **cd /tmp**

dir   List the contents of a directory on the remote system to the screen or to a file on the local system if you specify a local file name.

get   Copy the specified remote file to the specified local file. If you don't specify a local file name, then the remote file name will be used.

lcd   Change to the specified directory on the local host.

Example: **lcd /tmp**

ls   List the contents of a directory on the remote system to the screen or to a file on the local system if you specify a local file name.

mget   Copy multiple files from the remote host to the local host.

Example: **mget *.c**

put   Copy the specified local file to the specified remote file. If you don't specify a remote file name, then the local file name will be used.

Example: **put test.c**

mput   Copy multiple files from the local host to the remote host.

Example: **mput *.c**

system   Show the type of operating system running on the remote host.

Example: **system**

bye/quit   Close the connection to the remote host.

Example: **bye**

There are **ftp** commands in addition to those I have covered here.

telnet   Used for communication with another host using the telnet protocol. Telnet is an alternative to using **rlogin** described later. The following example show how to establish a telnet connection with the remote host system2.

	comments
$ telnet system2	
Connected to system2.	Telnet to system2
HP-UX system2	
login: **root**	Log in as root on system2
password:	Enter password
Welcome to system2.	
$	HP-UX prompt on system2

telnet - Communicate with another system using TELNET protocol.

The following list includes some commonly used **telnet** commands. This list is by no means complete.

open host   Open a connection to the specified host. I like to use the term system in place of host, but host is the official terminology. The system you specify can be either an official name or an alias you use to connect to the system.

close   After completing your **telnet** work you should terminate your connection with this command.

quit   This command closes any open TELNET sessions and exits you from **telnet**.

?   If you type only a "?" you get a help summary. If you type a "?" and a command name then you get help information about that command.

Berkeley Commands (Communication between UNIX Systems)

Berkeley commands are those used to communicate among UNIX systems. In environments with only HP-UX systems or HP-UX systems and those running other UNIX based operating systems, you have the option to use Berkeley commands.

Remote Copy (rcp)   This program is used to copy files and directories from one UNIX system to another. To copy the file **/tmp/krsort.c** from system1 to system2 you could do the following:

$ **rcp   system2:/tmp/krsort.c   /tmp/krsort.c**

In this example the user who issues the command is considered "equivalent" on both systems and has permission to copy files from one system to the other with **rcp**.

rcp - Remote file copy.

Options and Arguments:

           source file   This <u>argument</u> is the name of a file you wish to copy to a remote system or from a remote system.

      source directory   This <u>argument</u> is the name of a directory you wish to copy to a remote system or from a remote system.

      destination file   This <u>argument</u> is the file name to which a file will be copied.

destination directory   This <u>argument</u> is the directory name to which a directory will be copied.

              -p   This <u>option</u> preserves information about the source files. Such information as permissions and modification times are preserved for files copied.

              -r   This <u>option</u> performs a recursive copy. You can copy sub-directories of the source directory name using this option.

Remote login (rlogin) Supports login to a remote UNIX system. To remotely log in to system2 from system1 you would do the following:

$ rlogin system2

password:

Welcome to system2

$

If a password is requested when you issue the **rlogin** command, you are not equivalent on the two systems. If no password is requested, then you are indeed equivalent.

rlogin - Remote login.

Options and Arguments:

        remote host   This <u>argument</u> is the name of the remote host you wish to log in to.

        -l user name   This <u>option</u> allows you to specify the name of a user you wish to log in on the remote system.

Remote shell (remsh) With the **remsh** command you can sit on one HP-UX system and issue a command to be run remotely on a different HP-UX system and have the results displayed locally. In this case a **remsh** is issued to show a long listing of the file **/tmp/krsort.c**. The command is run on system2 but the result is displayed on system1 where the command was typed:

$ remsh system2 ll /tmp/krsort.c

-rwxrwxrwx 1 root sys 2896 Sept 1 10:54 /tmp/krsort.c

$

In this case the users on system1 and system2 must be equivalent or permission will be denied to issue this command.

remsh - Execute a command on a remote system.

Options and Arguments:

remote host   This <u>argument</u> is the name of the remote host on which you wish to run the command.

-l user name   This <u>option</u> allows you to specify the name of a user you wish to run the command as on the remote system.

Remote who (rwho)   Find out who is logged in on a remote UNIX system. Here is the output of issuing **rwho**:

$ rwho

root	system1:ttyu0	Sept 1 19:21
root	system2:console	Sept 1 13:17
tomd	system2:ttyp2	Sept 1 13:05

```
|         |      |            |       |-> time of login
|         |      |            |> day of login
|         |      |
|         |      |> terminal line
|         |> machine name
|
|> user name
```

For **rwho** to work, the **rwho** daemon (**rwhod**) must be running.

rwho - Show users logged in on remote systems.

___

Options and Arguments:

-l   This <u>option</u> will include in the output list users who have not typed any information in an hour or more. These users would otherwise be omitted.

Chapter 8

Shell Programming

Shell Programming

I am including this chapter on shell programming because I find that new HP-UX users often want to start writing simple shell programs right away. I can't cover shell programming in detail in just one chapter, but I can get you started on shell programming. It's not difficult at all to write simple shell programs and I'm sure you'll find this useful and be able to write your own shell programs.

There is much more to a shell than meets the eye. The shell is much more than the command line interpreter you saw in earlier chapters. UNIX shells actually provide a powerful interpretive programming language as well.

You may be asking yourself, "Why do I need to know about shell programming?" As a user you may find you can use shell programs to automate a lot of what you may be performing manually.

Using shell programs (sometimes called shell scripts), you can build many tools to automate tasks you perform on a regular basis. Using shell scripts, you can automate mundane tasks that require several commands to be executed sequentially. You can build new commands to perform such tasks as managing your files and directories. You could also build scripts that provide shortcuts for executing long or complex command lines.

The shell is one of the most powerful features on any UNIX system. If you can't find the right command to accomplish a task, you can probably build it quite easily using a shell script.

In this chapter I will show you the basic things you need to know to start programming in the Bourne shell. We will be covering the Bourne shell (as opposed to the Korn or C shells) because it is the simplest to program and it is a subset of the default HP-UX 10.x shell - the POSIX shell. Once you can program in the Bourne shell, it is easy to adapt to the other available shells and all Bourne shell programs will run in the POSIX shell. The POSIX shell has everything you need as a user, so I strongly suggest you use this shell.

The best way to learn shell programming is by example. There are many examples given in this chapter. Some serve no purpose other than to demonstrate the current topic. Most, however, are useful tools or parts of tools that you can easily expand and adapt into your environment. The examples provide easy to understand prompts and output messages. Most examples show what is needed to provide the functionality we are after. They do not do a great deal of error checking. From my experience, however, it only takes a few minutes to get a shell program to do what you want; it can take hours to handle every situation and every error condition. Therefore, these programs are not very dressed up (maybe a sport coat versus a tuxedo). I'm giving you what you need to know to build some useful tools for your environment. I hope you will have enough knowledge and interest by the time we get to the end of this section to learn and do more.

Bourne Shell Programming

A shell program is simply a file containing a set of commands you wish to execute sequentially. The file needs to be set with execute permissions so you can execute it just by typing the name of the script.

There are two basic forms of shell programs:

1. Simple command files - When you have a command line or set of command lines that you use over and over, you can use one simple command to execute them all.

2. Structured programs - The shell provides much more than the ability to "batch" together a series of commands. It has many of the features that any higher level programming language contains:

   - Variables for storing data

   - Decision-making controls (the **if** and **case** commands)

   - Looping abilities (the **for** and **while** loops)

   - Function calls for modularity

Given these two basic forms you can build everything from simple command replacements to much larger and more complex data manipulations.

Here is a simple shell script example:

```
#!/bin/sh
# This is a simple shell program that displays today's date
# in a short message.
echo "Today's date is"
date +%x
```

Before we go on let's take a look at what each line does.

```
#!/bin/sh
```

The different shells (Bourne, POSIX, Korn, and C) do not use all the same commands. Each has some commands that work differently or don't work at all in other shells. Simple commands like those in this script will work in all shells, but there are many cases where that is not true.

Normally, when you run a shell program, the system tries to execute commands using the same shell you are using for your interactive command lines. This line makes sure the system knows that this is a Bourne shell (**/bin/sh**) script so it can start a Bourne shell to execute the commands. Note that the **#!** must be the very first two characters in the file.

If we don't include this line, someone running a shell other than the Bourne shell might have unexpected results when trying to run one of our programs.

As a good practice you should include **#!shellname** as the first line of every shell program you write. This, however, is an area where there is a change between HP-UX 10.x and HP-UX 9.x. Keep in mind that the default shell in HP-UX 10.x is the POSIX shell. Table 8-1 shows the locations of the most commonly used shells in HP-UX 10.x.

Table 8-1 Shell Locations

Shell Name	Location
POSIX shell	/usr/bin/sh
C shell	/usr/bin/csh
Bourne shell	/usr/old/bin/sh
Korn shell	/usr/bin/ksh

Note that I claimed I was giving you an example of a Bourne shell program yet I used **#!/bin/sh** and this does not appear in the table for any shell. **/bin/sh** is the HP-UX 9.x location for the Bourne shell. If indeed you are writing a Bourne shell program, you should use the new location of the Bourne shell (**/usr/old/bin/sh**) in your Bourne shell programs. I would, however, recommend you use the new POSIX shell for your shell programs and since the POSIX shell is a superset of the Bourne shell, then all of the information in this section applies to both the Bourne and POSIX shells. My program that begins with a **#!/bin/sh** does work, however. This is because the HP-UX 10.x designers provided a link from the old Bourne shell path to the new path. Because this is a potentially confusing area and there is a lot of HP-UX 10.x and 9.x compatibility built-in, it's worth taking a quick look at the characteristics of these shell programs.

```
$ ll -i /usr/bin/sh

   603 -r-xr-xr-x 2 bin bin 405504 Dec 12 03:00 /usr/bin/sh

$ ll -i /bin/sh

   603 -r-xr-xr-x 2 bin bin 405504 Dec 12 03:00 /bin/sh
```

This long listing, with the "-i" option to give me the inode number of
the file, proves to be quite revealing. The POSIX shell **/usr/bin/sh** and the
Bourne shell **/usr/bin** have the same inode number. Even though I think I
am running the Bourne shell when I type **#!/bin/sh** I am actually running
the POSIX shell **/usr/bin/sh**. Because I hate to be behind the times I think
I'll continue typing **#!/bin/sh** and therefore be running the POSIX shell.
You can take this analysis one step further and look at the Bourne shell:

```
$ ll -i /usr/old/bin/sh

 16518 -r-xr-xr-x 1 bin bin 200704 Dec 12 03:00/bin/old/bin/sh
```

Here we can see that the old Bourne shell is indeed a different program, with a different inode number, and a different size. I would not recommend you use this shell.

There is also an **/sbin/sh** that my system uses when it boots because
the **/usr/bin/sh** file may not be mounted at the time of boot.

Now, getting back to Bourne shell programming, let's continue looking at our example.

```
# This is a simple shell program that displays today's date
# in a short message.
```

These are comments. Everything after a # in a command line is considered a comment. (**#!** on the first line is the one very big exception.)

```
echo "Today's date is"
```

The **echo** command generates prompts and messages in shell programs. See the echo(1) manual entry to see all of the options available with echo for formatting your output. We commonly enclose the string to be displayed in double quotes. In this case we did it because we needed to let the shell know that the apostrophe was part of the string and not a single quote that needs a match.

```
date
```

Executes the **date** command.

After we have the commands in the file, we need to make the file executable:

```
$ chmod +x today
```

The "$" is the default Bourne shell command line prompt. Changing the permissions this way makes the file executable by anyone. You will only need to do this once after creating the file. See chmod(1) if you need more information on setting permissions.

To execute our new script, we type its name, as shown below:

```
$ today
Today's date is
01/27/93
$
```

Here is a more complex example:

```
#!/bin/sh
# This is a simple shell program that displays the current
# directory name before a long file listing (ll) of that
# directory.
# The script name is myll
echo "Long listing of directory:"
pwd
echo
ll
```

This is what **myll** looks like when it runs:

```
$ myll
Long listing of directory:
/tmp
total 14398
-rw------- 1 gerry  users  47104  Jan 27 21:09 Ex01816
-rw-rw-rw- 1 root   root       0  Jan 27 09:17 test
-rw-r--r-- 1 ralph  users  14336  Jan 21 15:05 poetry
-rw-r--r-- 1 root   other  66272  Jan 27 10:51 up.log
```

Before we can create more complex shell programs we need to learn more about some of the programming features built into the shell.

Shell Variables

A shell variable is similar to a variable in any programming language. A variable is simply a name you give to a storage location. Unlike most languages, however, you never have to declare or initialize your variables, you just use them.

Shell variables can have just about any name that starts with a letter (uppercase or lowercase). To avoid confusion with special shell characters (like filename generation characters), keep the names simple and use just letters, numbers, and underscore (_).

To assign values to shell variables you simply type

```
name=value
```

Note that there are no spaces before and after the = character.

Here are some examples of setting shell variables from the command line. These examples work correctly.

```
$ myname=ralph
$ HerName=mary
```

This one does not work because of the space after "his:".

```
$ his name=norton
his: not found
```

The shell assumes that "his" is a command and tries to execute it. The rest of the line is ignored.

This example contains an illegal character (+) in the name:

```
$ one+one=two
one+one=two: not found
```

A variable must start with a letter:

```
$ 3word=hi
3word=hi: not found
```

Now that we can store values in our variables we need to know how to use those values. The dollar sign ($) is used to get the value of a variable. Any time the shell sees a $ in the command line, it assumes that the characters immediately following it are a variable name. It replaces the $variable with its value. Here are some simple examples using variables at the command line:

```
$ myname=ralph
$ echo myname
myname
$ echo $myname
ralph
$ echo $abc123
```

In the first **echo** command there is no $, so the shell ignores **myname** and **echo** gets **myname** as an argument to be echoed. In the second **echo**, however, the shell sees the $, looks up the value of **myname,** and puts it on the command line. Now **echo** sees **ralph** as its argument (not **myname** or $**myname**). The final **echo** statement is similar except that we have not given a value to **abc123** so the shell assumes it has no value and replaces $**abc123** with nothing. Therefore **echo** has no arguments and echos a blank line.

There may be times when you want to concatenate variables and strings. This is very easy to do in the shell:

```
$ myname=ralph
$ echo "My name is $myname"
My name is ralph
```

There may be times when the shell can become confused if the variable name is not easily identified in the command line:

```
$ string=dobeedobee
$ echo "$stringdoo"
```

We wanted to display "dobeedobeedoo" but the shell thought the variable name was stringdoo, which had no value. To accomplish this we can use curly braces around the variable name to separate it from surrounding characters:

```
$ echo "${string}doo"
dobeedobeedoo
```

You can set variables in shell programs in the same way, but you would also like to do things such as save the output of a command in a variable so you can use it later. You may want to ask users a question and read their response into a variable so you can examine it.

Command Substitution

Command substitution allows us to save the output from a command (**std-out**) into a shell variable. To demonstrate this, let's take another look at how our "today" example can be done using command substitution.

```
#!/bin/sh
d=`date +%x`
echo "Today's date is $d"
```

The back quotes (`) around the **date** command tell the shell to execute date and place its output on the command line. The output will then be assigned to the variable **d**.

```
$ today
Today's date is 01/27/93
```

We could also have done this without using the variable **d**. We could have just included the **date** command in the echo string:

```
#!/bin/sh
echo "Today's date is `date +%x`"
```

Reading User Input

The most common way to get information from the user is to prompt him or her and then read their response. The **echo** command is most commonly used to display the prompt; then the **read** command is used to read a line of input from the user (**stdin**). Words from the input line can be assigned to one or several shell variables.

Here is an example with comments to show you how **read** can be used:

```
#!/bin/sh
```

```
# program: readtest
echo "Please enter your name: \c" # the \c leaves cursor on
                                  # this line.
read name # there is no $ because we are doing an assignment
          # of whatever the user enters into name.
echo "Hello, $name"
echo "Please enter your two favorite colors: \c"
read color1 color2 # first word entered goes into color1
                   # remainder of line goes into color2
echo "You entered $color2 and $color1"
```

If we ran this program it would look something like this:

```
$ readtest
Please enter your name: gerry
Hello, gerry
Please enter your two favorite colors: blue green
You entered green and blue
$
```

Notice how the **read** command assigned the two words entered for colors into the two respective color variables. If the user entered fewer words than the read command was expecting, the remaining variables would be set to null. If the user enters too many words, all extra words entered are assigned into the last variable. This is how you can get a whole line of input into one variable. Here's an example of what would happen if you entered more than two colors:

```
$ readtest
Please enter your name: gerry
Hello, gerry
Please enter your two favorite colors: chartreuse orchid blue
You entered orchid blue and chartreuse
$
```

Arguments to Shell Programs

Shell programs can have command line arguments just like any regular command. Command line arguments used when you invoke your shell program are stored in a special set of variables. These are called the positional parameters.

The first ten words on the command line are directly accessible in the shell program using the special variables **$0-$9**. This is how they work:

$0   The command name

$1   The first argument

$2   The second argument

$3   .

               .

               .

$9   The ninth argument

If you are not sure how many command line arguments you may get when your program is run, there are two other variables that can help:

$#   The number of command line arguments

$*   A space-separated list of all of the command line arguments
         (which does not include the command name)

The variable **$*** is commonly used with the **for** loop (soon to be explained) to process shell script command lines with any number of arguments.

Figure 8-1 illustrates some simple examples of using arguments in our shell programs:

```
#!/bin/sh
# This is a simple shell program that takes one command line
# argument (a directory name) then displays the full pathname
# of that directory before doing a long file listing (ll) on
# it.
#
# The script name is myll
cd $1
echo "Long listing of the `pwd` directory:"
echo
ll
```

Figure 8-1   **myll** Shell Program

If we run **myll** with a directory name, the script changes directory, echoes the message containing the full pathname (notice the command substitution), then executes the **ll** command.

Note that the **cd** in the **myll** program will change only the working directory of the script; it does not affect the working directory of the shell we run **myll** from.

```
$ myll /tmp
Long listing of the /tmp directory:
total 380
drwxrwxrwx 2 bin    sys     1024 Feb 1 15:01 files
-rw-rw-rw- 1 root   root       0 Feb 1 13:07 ktl_log
-rw-rw-rw- 1 root   root       0 Feb 1 13:07 ntl_lib.log
-rw-rw-rw- 1 root   root     115 Feb 1 13:07 ntl.read
-rw-r--r-- 1 root other 108008 Feb 2 08:42 database.log
-r-xr--r-- 1 root other    466 Feb 1 15:29 updist.scr
```

In this case we could give **myll** no argument and it would still work properly. If we don't provide any command line arguments, then **$1** will be null so nothing goes on the command line after **cd**. This will make **cd** take us to our home directory and perform the **ll** there.

If we provide more than one argument, only the first is used and any others are ignored.

If we use a command line argument it MUST be a directory name; otherwise the **cd** command fails and the script terminates with a "bad directory" error message. Later I will show how to test for valid directory and file names so you can work around potential errors.

A more complex example can be used to build new versions of the **ps** command. Below are two examples that use command line arguments and command substitution to help you with your process management.

The **psg** shell program in Figure 8-2 is handy for searching through what is typically a long process status listing to find only certain commands or user processes. These examples use **grep**. **grep** finds all lines that contain the pattern you are searching for.

```
#!/bin/sh
# Program name: psg
# Usage: psg some_pattern
#
# This program searches through a process status (ps -ef)
# listing for a pattern given as the first command line
# argument.
procs='ps -ef`                      # Get the process listing
head=`echo "$procs" | line`         # Take off the first line (the
                                    # headings)
echo "$head"                        # Write out the headings
echo "$procs" | grep -i $1 | grep -v $0 # Write out lines
    # containing $1 but not this program's command line

# Note that $procs MUST be quoted or the newlines in the ps
# -ef listing will be turned into spaces when echoed. $head
# must also be quoted to preserve any extra white space.
```

Figure 8-2   **psg** Shell Program

Here's what **psg** looks like when it runs. In this example we want to look at all of the Korn shells running on the system.

```
$ psg ksh
    UID    PID   PPID  C   STIME       TTY   TIME   COMMAND
   root   1258   1252  0   18:00:34   ttyp1   0:00   ksh
   root   1347   1346  0   18:03:15   ttyp2   0:01   ksh
  ralph   1733   1732  0   20:06:11   ttys0   0:00   -ksh
```

In this example we want to see all the processes that **ralph** is running:

```
$ psg ralph
    UID    PID   PPID  C   STIME       TTY   TIME   COMMAND
  ralph   1733   1732  0   20:06:11   ttys0   0:00   -ksh
```

```
ralph  1775  1733  0  20:07:43  ttys0  0:00  vi afile
```

This program also works to find terminal, process ID, parent process ID, start date, and any other information from **ps**.

The **gkill** shell program in Figure 8-3 searches through a **ps -ef** listing for a pattern (just like **psg**); then it kills all listed processes. The examples use the **cut** command, which allows you to specify a range of columns to retain.

```
#!/bin/sh
# Program name: gkill
# Usage: gkill some_pattern
# This program will find all processes that contain the
# pattern specified as the first command line argument then
# kills those processes.
# get the process listing
procs=`ps -ef`
echo "The following processes will be killed:"
# Here we list the processes to kill. We don't kill this
# process
echo "$procs" | grep -i $1 | grep -v $0
# Allow the user a chance to cancel.
echo "\nPress Return to continue Ctrl-C to exit"
# If the user presses Ctrl-C the program will exit.
# Otherwise this read waits for the next return character and
# continue.
read junk
# find the pattern and cut out the pid field
pids=`echo "$procs" | grep -i $1 | grep -v $0 | cut -c9-15`
# kill the processes
kill $pids
```

Figure 8-3   gkill Shell Program

If we don't provide any command line arguments, **grep** issues an error and the program continues. In the next section we will learn how to check if **$1** is set and how to gracefully clean up if it's not.

Here is an example of running **gkill**:

```
$ gkill xclock
```

```
The following processes will be killed:
   marty 3145 3016 4 15:06:59 ttyp5 0:00 xclock
```

```
Press return to continue Ctrl-C to exit

[1] + Terminated                    xclock &
```

Testing and Branching

Decision making is one of the shell's most powerful features. There are two ways to check conditions and branch to a piece of code that can handle that condition.

For example, you may want to ask the user a question and then check if the answer was *yes* or *no*. You may also want to check if a file exists before you operate on it. In either case you can use the **if** command to accomplish the task. Here are a few shell script segments that explain each part of the **if** command:

```
echo "Continue? \c"
read ans
if [ "$ans" = "n" ]
then
      echo "Goodbye"
      exit
fi
```

The **echo** and **read** provide a prompt and response as usual. The **if** statement executes the next command and if it succeeds, it executes any commands between the **then** and the **fi** (if spelled backwards).

Note that the **\c** in the **echo** command suppresses the new line that **echo** normally generates. This leaves the cursor on the line immediately after the "Continue? " prompt. This is commonly used when prompting for user input.

The **test** command is the most common command to use with the **if** command. The ["$ans" = "n"] is the **test** command. It performs many types of file, string, and numeric logical tests and if the condition is true, the test succeeds.

The syntax of the **test** command requires spaces around the [ ] or you will get a syntax error when the program runs. Also, notice the double quotes around the response variable **$ans**. This is a strange anomaly with the **test** command. If the user presses only [[RETURN]] at the prompt without typing any other character, the value of **$ans** will be null. If we didn't have the quote marks around **$ans** in the **test** command, it would look like this when the value of **$ans** was substituted into the test command:

```
[ = "n" ]
```

This would generate a "test: argument expected" error when you run the program. This is a very common mistake and if you ever get this error, you should look for variables in your **test** commands with null values.

There is another form of the **if** command that is very common. It allows you to do one thing if a condition is met or do something else if not:

```
if [    ]              # if some condition is true
then
                       # do something
else
                       # otherwise do this
fi
```

There are many conditions that the **test** command can test as shown in Table 8-2.

Table 8-2   test Command Conditions

String tests:

["$a" = "string"]	True if $a is equal to "string"
["$a" != "string"]	True if $a is NOT equal to "string"
[-z "$a"]	True if $a is null (zero characters)

Table 8-2 **test** Command Conditions

String tests:

[-n "$a"]	True if $a is NOT null

Numeric tests:

[$x -eq 1]	True if $x is equal to 1
[$x -ne 1]	True if $x is NOT equal to 1
[$x -lt 1]	True if $x is less than 1
[$x -gt 1]	True if $x is greater than 1
[$x -le 1]	True if $x is less than or equal to 1
[$x -ge 1]	True if $x is greater than or equal to 1

File tests:

[-d $file]	True if $file is a directory
[-f $file]	True if $file is a file
[-s $file]	True if $file is a file with > 0 bytes
[-r $file]	True if $file is readable
[-w $file]	True if $file is writable
[-x $file]	True if $file is executable

Tests can be combined using **-a** to logically "AND" the tests together, **-o** to logically "OR" two tests, and **!** to "negate" a test. For example, this test statement is true only if the **$interactive** variable is set to true or **$file** is a directory:

```
[ "$interactive" = "TRUE" -o -d $file ]
```

Here is a useful extension to the **gkill** program earlier shown. It checks to see that we have exactly one command line argument before the program will attempt to do the processing. It uses a numeric test and the $# variable, which represents the number of command line arguments. It should be inserted before any other lines of code in the **gkill** example given above.

```
# If we don't have exactly one command line argument write an
# error and exit.
if [ $# -ne 1 ]
then
    echo "Usage: $0 pattern"
    echo "Some pattern matching the processes to kill must
    echo "be specified"
    exit 1 # Exit 1 terminates the program and tells the
           # calling shell that we had an error.
fi
```

Some other possible extensions to the **gkill** program might be to:

- Allow yourself to specify a signal to use with the **kill** command. For example:
  gkill -9 ralph
  would find all of ralph's processes and then kill them with **kill -9**.

- Make sure that a valid message is printed if we can't find any processes to kill using the specified pattern.

This same type of command line check is easily applied to the **psg** program to make sure you have exactly one argument representing the pattern to search for.

When you are reading user input, you may want to check if the user entered a value at all. If they didn't, you would provide a reasonable default value. This is easily done with a variable modifier.

This example reads answer ("ans") from the user and then checks its value using an **if** command:

```
echo "Do you really want to remove all of your files? \c"
read ans
if [ ${ans:-n} = y ]
then
    rm -rf *
fi
```

The **${ans:-n}** statement checks the value of **$ans**. If there is a value in **$ans,** use it in the command line. If the user simply pressed [[RETURN]] at the prompt, **$ans** will be null. In this case **${ans:-n}** will evaluate to n when we do the comparison. Basically, in one small statement it says, "if the user did not provide an answer, assume he meant n".

There is another modifier that is often used:

```
${var:=default}
```

It returns the value of **var** if it is set; it returns the default if **var** is not set and it will also assign the default as the value of **var** for future use.

All of the modifiers available in the Bourne shell are in the **sh** manual entry.

Making Decisions with the case Statement

The **case** statement is another way to make decisions and test conditions in shell programs. It is most commonly used to check for certain patterns in command line arguments. For example, if you wanted to determine if the first command line argument is an option (starts with a -), the **case** statement is the easiest way to do that. The **case** statement is also used to respond to different user input (such as asking the user to select a choice from a menu).

The **case** statement is probably one of the most complicated shell commands because of its syntax:

```
case pattern_to_match in
        pattern1)  cmdA
                   cmdB
```

```
                        ;;
        pattern2)  cmdC
                        ;;
                    ...
        *)  cmdZ
                        ;;
    esac
```

pattern_to_match is usually a shell variable that you are testing (like a command line argument or a user response). If **pattern_to_match** matches **pattern1,** then commands **cmdA** and **cmdB** are executed. The **;;** separates this pattern's command list from the next pattern. In all cases, when **;;** is reached, the program jumps to the **esac** (**case** spelled backwards).

If **pattern_to_match** matches **pattern2,** then **cmdC** is executed and we jump to **esac**, the end of the **case** statement.

The ***** is provided so if **pattern_to_match** did not match anything else, it will execute **cmdZ**. It's important to have a default action to handle the case where the user types an invalid entry.

For more robust pattern matching any file name generation characters (*, [ ], ?) can be used to do special pattern matches. There is also a very useful way to check for multiple patterns in one line using the | symbol which means logical "OR". Here's an example:

```
echo "Do you want to continue? (y/n) \c"
read ans
case $ans in
    y|Y) echo "Continuing"
                ...
        ;;
    n|N) echo "Done, Goodbye"
        exit
        ;;
    *) echo "Invalid input"
        ;;
esac
```

Here is another example where we are testing to see if **$1** (the first command line argument) is a valid option (a character we recognize that begins with a -).

```
case $1 in
        -l | -d) # Perform a listing
                echo "All files in $HOME:\n"
                ll -R $HOME | more
                ;;
        -i) # -i means set an interactive flag to true
            interactive="TRUE"
                ;;
        *)  # Invalid input
            echo "$0: $1 is an invalid option"
            exit 1
            ;;
esac
```

A **case** statement similar to this is used in the **trash** program at the end of this chapter.

Looping

There are many times when you want to perform an action repeatedly. In the shell there are two ways to do this:

1. The **for** loop takes a list of items and performs the commands in the loop once for each item in the list.

2. The **while** loop executes some commands (usually the **test** command) if that command executes successfully. (If the test condition is true, then the commands in the loop are executed and then the command is again executed to see if we should loop again.)

The basic format of the **for** loop is:

```
for var in list_of_items
do
        cmdA
        cmdB
        cmdC
done
```

When the loop starts, the variable **var** has its value set to the first word in the **list_of_items** to loop through. Then, the three commands between the **do** and the **done** statements are executed. After the program reaches the **done** statement, it goes back to the top of the loop and assigns **var** to the next item in the list, executes the commands, and so on. The last time through the loop, the program continues with the next executable statement after the **done** statement.

Let's look at an example to copy certain files to several machines using the **rcp** command and verify that they got there using the **remsh** command:

```
for host in neptune jupiter mars earth sun
do
     echo $host
     rcp /home/denise/.mailrc /home/denise/.lrom $host:/home/denise
     remsh $host ll /home/denise
done
```

You can also process lists of files in the current directory using command substitution to generate the **list_of_items**:

```
for file in `ls`
do
     if [ -r $file ]
     then
             echo "$file is readable"
     fi
done
```

Note that **for file in *** would have done the same thing.

If you have a large list of things you would like to loop through and you don't want to type them on the command line, you can enter them in a file instead. Then, using the **cat** command and command substitution, you can generate the **list_of_items**:

```
for i in `cat important_files`
do
```

```
      # do something with each of the files listed in the
      # important_files file.
done
```

The **for** loop, however, is most commonly used to process the list of command line arguments (**$***):

```
for name in $*
do
      if [ ! -f $name -a ! -d $name ]
      then
          echo "$name is not a valid file or directory name"
      else
        # do something with the file or directory
      fi
done
```

The **trash** program contains a **for** loop that processes command line arguments in a similar way.

The while Loop

The **while** loop has the following format:

```
while cmd1
do
        cmdA
        cmdB
        cmdC
done
```

cmd1 is executed first. If it executes successfully, then the commands between the **do** and the **done** statements are executed. **cmd1** is then executed again; if successful, the commands in the loop are executed again, and so on. When **cmd1** fails, the program jumps past the **done** statement and resumes execution with the next executable statement.

Most of the time the command executed in place of **cmd1** is the **test** command. You can then perform logical tests as described in the **if** section.

If the test succeeds (is true), the commands in the loop are executed and the script tests the condition again. The **while** loop is useful if you have a fixed number of times you want the loop to run or if you want something to happen until some condition is met.

The **expr** command is the only way we can do math in the Bourne shell. (The Korn and C shells have some math functions built in). The line

```
expr $i + 1
```

takes the current value of the variable **i** (which must be an integer or the **expr** command will complain) and adds 1 to it, writing the result to standard output (stdout). By using the **expr** command with command substitution, we can capture the result and assign it back into **i**. This is how we increment variables in the shell. The **expr** command can also perform integer subtraction, multiplication, division, remainder, and matching functions. See the **expr** manual entry for all of the details.

The **while** loop can also be used to process command line arguments one at a time, using the number of command line arguments and the **shift** command:

```
while [ $# -ne 0 ]
do
    case $1 in
    -*) # $1 must be an option because it starts with -
        # Add it to the list of options:
        opts="$opts $1"
        ;;
     *) # $1 must be an argument. Add it to the list of
        # command line arguments:
        args="$args $1"
        ;;
  esac
  shift
done
```

The **shift** command shifts the remaining arguments in **$*** to the left by one position and decrements **$#**. What was the first argument (**$1**) is now gone forever; what was in **$2** is now in **$1**, and so on. In the process of shifting command line arguments, **$#** is also decremented to accurately reflect the number of arguments left in **$***.

You may want some commands to run until the user stops the program or until some stop condition is met. An infinite **while** loop is the best way to do this. For example, let's say we are prompting users for some input and we will continue to prompt them until they give us valid input:

```
while true
do
    # prompt users and get their response
    echo "Enter yes or no: \c"
    read ans

    # Check if the response is valid
    if [ "$ans" = "yes" -o "$ans" = "no" ]
    then
    # If it is valid, stop the looping
    break
  else
    # Otherwise print an error message and try it again
    # from the top of the loop
    echo "Invalid input, try again!\n"
  fi
done
# Now that we have valid input we can process the user's
# request
    .
    .
    .
```

true is a special command that always executes successfully. The loop does not terminate unless the user stops the program by killing it or until a **break** command is executed in the loop. The **break** command will stop the loop.

Shell Functions

As you write shell programs, you will notice that there are certain sets of commands that appear in many places within a program. For example, several times in a script you may check user input and issue an appropriate message if input is invalid. It can be tedious to type the same lines of code in your program numerous times. It can be a nuisance if you later want to change these lines.

Instead, you can you can put these commands into a shell function. Functions look and act like a new command that can be used inside the script. Here's an example of a basic shell function:

```
# This is a function that may be called from anywhere within
# the program. It displays a standard usage error message
# then exits the program.

print_usage()
{
    echo "Usage:"
    echo "To trash files: $0 [-i] files_to_trash..."
    echo "Display trashed files: $0 -d"
    echo "Remove all trashed files: $0 -rm"
    echo "Print this message: $0 -help"
    exit 1
}
```

print_usage is now a new command in your shell program. You can use it anywhere in this script.

Shell functions also have their own set of positional parameters (**$1-$9, $#,** and **$***) so you can pass them arguments just like any other command. The only nuance is that **$0** represents the name of the shell program, not the name of the function.

This shell function is used several times in the **trash** program example.

Figure 8-4 is a fairly complex program that exercises all of the concepts we have covered so far. It is a **trash** program that removes files from their original locations. Instead of removing them permanently, it places

them in a trash can in your home directory. This is a fairly robust program,
but I'm sure you can think of many extensions as you read through it.

```
#!/bin/sh
# Program name: trash
# Usage:
#  To trash files:    trash [-i] file_names_to_trash ...
#  Display trashed files:    trash -d
#  Remove all trashed files: trash -rm
#  Print a help message:    trash -help

# This program takes any number of directory or file name
# arguments. If the argument is a file it will be removed
# from its current place in the file system and placed in the
# user's trash directory ($HOME/.trash). If the argument is a
# directory name the program will ask if the user really
# wants to trash the whole directory.
#
# This program also takes a -i (interactive) option. Like
# the rm command, if the -i is the first argument on the
# command line, the program stops and asks if each file
# named in the remaining arguments should be trashed.

#
# The -d (display) option shows the contents of the
# user's trashed files.
#
# The -help option displays a usage message for the user.
```

Figure 8-4 **trash** Shell Program

```
# The -rm (remove) option interactively
# asks the user if each file or directory in the trash
# directory should be removed permanently.
#
# The -h, -d and -rm options may not be used with
# any other command line arguments.

# Possible extensions:
# - Enhance the -rm option to remove a list of files
# from the trash directory from the command line.
# - Create a program to be run by cron once nightly to empty
# everyone's trash directory.

# This is a function that may be called from anywhere within
# the program. It displays a standard usage error message
# then exits the program.
print_usage()
{
  echo "Usage:"
  echo "To trash files: $0 [-i] file_names_to_trash ..."
  echo "Display trashed files:    $0 -d"
  echo "Remove all trashed files: $0 -rm"
  echo "Print this message:       $0 -help"
exit 1
}
# Make sure we have at least one command line argument before
# we start.
if [ $# -lt 1 ]
then
    print_usage
fi

# If this flag is true then we need to do interactive
# processing.
interactive="FALSE"

# This is the name of the trash can.
trash_dir="$HOME/.trash"

# Make sure the trash directory exists before we go any
# further.
if [ ! -d $trash_dir ]
then
    mkdir $trash_dir
fi
# Sort out the command line arguments.
case $1 in
   -help) # Print a help message.
      print_usage
      ;;
```

Figure 8-4   trash Shell Program (Continued)

```
 -d | -rm) # a -d or -rm were given
        # If it was not the only command line argument
        # then display a usage message and then exit.
        if [ $# -ne 1 ]
        then
            print_usage
        fi

        # Otherwise do the task requested.
        if [ $1 = "-d" ]
        then
            echo "The contents of $trash_dir:\n"
            ll -R $trash_dir | more
        else
            # remove all files from the trash directory
            rm -rf $trash_dir/*
            # get any dotfiles too
            rm -rf $trash_dir/.[!.]*
        fi

        # Now we can exit successfully.
        exit 0
        ;;
 -i) # If the first argument is -i ask about each file as it
        # is processed.
        interactive="TRUE"
        # Take -i off the command line so we know that the
        # rest of the arguments are file or directory names.

        shift
        ;;

  -*)# Check for an option we don't understand.
        echo "$1 is not a recognized option."
        print_usage
        ;;
        esac

# Just for fun we'll keep a count of the files that were
# trashed.
count=0

for file in $*
do
 # First make sure the file or directory to be renamed exists.
 # If it doesn't, add it to a list of bad files to be written
 # out later. Otherwise process it.
 if [ ! -f $file -a ! -d $file ]
 then
     bad_files="$bad_files $file"
 else
# If we are in interactive mode ask for confirmation
# on each file. Otherwise ask about directories.
```

Figure 8-4   trash Shell Program (Continued)

```
if [ "$interactive" = "TRUE" -o -d $file ]
then
    # Ask the user for confirmation (default answer is no).
    if [ -d $file ]
    then
       echo "Do you want to trash the dir $file ? (y/n) n\b\c"
    else
       echo "Do you really want to trash $file ? (y/n) n\b\c"
    fi
    read doit

    # If they answered y then do the move.
    # Otherwise print a message that the file was not touched.
    if [ "${doit:-n}" = y ]
    then
         mv -i $file $trash_dir
         echo "$file was trashed to $trash_dir"
         count='expr $count + 1'
    else
         echo "$file was not trashed"
    fi
  else # We are not in interactive mode, so just do it.
       mv -i $file $trash_dir count='expr
       $count + 1'
  fi
fi
done

echo "$0: trashed $count item(s)"

if [ -n "$bad_files" ]
then
    echo "The following name(s) do not exist and \c"
    echo "could not be trashed:"
    echo "$bad_files"
fi

exit 0
```

Figure 8-4   **trash** Shell Program (Continued)

awk in Shell Programs

awk is a very powerful symbolic programming language. A WHAT?

Simply stated, **awk** searches for patterns in lines of input (from stdin or from a file) For each line that matches the specified pattern, it can perform some very complex processing on that line. The code to actually process matching lines of input is a cross between a shell script and a C program.

Data manipulation tasks that would be very complex with combinations of **grep**, **cut,** and **paste** are very easily done with **awk**. Since **awk** is a programming language, it can also perform mathematical operations or check the input very easily. (Shells don't do math very well.) It can even do floating-point math. (Shells deal only with integers and strings.)

The basic form of an **awk** program looks like this:

```
awk '/pattern_to_match/ { program to run }' input_file_names
```

Notice that the whole program is enclosed in single quotes. If no input file names are specified, **awk** reads from **stdin** (as from a pipe).

The **pattern_to_match** must appear between the **/** characters. The pattern is actually called a regular expression. Some common regular expression examples are shown in the examples.

The program to execute is written in **awk** code, which looks something like C. The program is executed whenever a line of input matches the **pattern_to_match**. If **/pattern_to_match/** does not precede the program in **{ }**, then the program is executed for every line of input.

awk works with fields of the input lines. Fields are words separated by white spaces. The fields in **awk** patterns and programs are referenced with **$**, followed by the field number. For example, the second field of an input line is **$2**. If you are using an **awk** command in your shell programs, the fields (**$1**, **$2**, etc.) are not confused with the shell scripts positional parameters, because the **awk** variables are enclosed in single quotes so the shell ignores them.

But let's not talk about it! Let's see some examples.

This simple example lists just the terminals that are active on your system (the terminal name is the second field of a **who** listing):

```
who | awk '{ print $2 }'
```

Note that **cut** could have done this also, but you would have had to know exactly which columns the terminal name occupied in the **who** output as shown below:

```
who | cut -c12-20
```

If the user or terminal name is longer than normal in any line, this command will not work. The **awk** example will work because it looks at fields, not columns.

In our **gkill** example, we used **grep** and **cut** to find the process IDs of the processes to kill:

```
procs=`ps -ef`
procs_to_kill=`echo "$procs" | grep -i $1`
pids=`echo "$procs_to_kill" | cut -c9-15`
```

These three complex commands can be replaced with one **awk** command:

```
pids=`ps -ef | awk '/'$1'/ { print $2 } ' `
```

The $1 is actually outside the single quotes, so it is interpreted by the shell as the first command line argument.

The **llsum** program shown in Figure 8-5 is a more complex example. A few things to note:

- **BEGIN** is a special pattern that means execute the **awk** program in {} before the first line of input. It is usually used for initializing variables and printing headers on the output.
- **END** is used after the last line of input, generally for summarizing the input.
- **printf** is a formatted print statement, as in C. The first argument is a format string containing what you want to print. It contains special

characters for printing different things such as

%**s** means we are printing a string

%**d** means we are printing an integer

%**f** means we are printing a floating-point number

- The **$1 ~ /pattern/** says: IF the first field matches the pattern, then do the program in {}.

```
#!/bin/sh
# Program: llsum
# Usage: llsum files_or_directories_to_summarize
#
# Displays a truncated long listing (ll) and displays size
# statistics of the files in the listing.
# A sample long listing for reference. Notice that the first
# line of output is less than 8 fields long and is not
# processed.
# ll
# total 46
# drwxrwxrwx 2 gerry aec 24            Mar 21 18:25  awk_ex
# crw--w--w- 1 root  sys 0 0x000000    Mar 22 15:32  /dev/con
#
# awk field numbers:
#     $1      $2 $3    $4  $5              $6  $7  $8      $9
ll $* | \
awk ' BEGIN { x=i=0; printf "%-16s%-10s%8s%8s\n",\
                  "FILENAME","OWNER","SIZE","TYPE" }

# Print out the owner, size, and type. Then sum the size.
$1 ~ /^[-dlps]/  { # line format for normal files
          printf "%-16s%-10s%8d",$9,$3,$5
          x = x + $5
          i++
          }

# If the line starts with a - it's a regular file; d is
# directory, etc.
  $1 ~ /^-/ { printf "%8s\n","file" } # standard file types
  $1 ~ /^d/ { printf "%8s\n","dir" }
  $1 ~ /^l/ { printf "%8s\n","link" }
  $1 ~ /^p/ { printf "%8s\n","pipe" }
  $1 ~ /^s/ { printf "%8s\n","socket" }
  $1 ~ /^[bc]/ {         # line format for device files
               printf "%-16s%-10s%8s%8s\n",$10,$3,"","dev"
               }

END
{ printf "\nThese files occupy %d bytes (%.4f Mbytes)\n",\
 x, x / (1024*1024)
    printf "Average file size is %d bytes\n", x/i
}' | \
more # Pipe the output through the more command so it will
      # page.
```

Figure 8-5 llsum Shell Program

The following is an example of running **llsum**:

```
$ llsum /users/tomd
FILENAME            OWNER         SIZE    TYPE

.Xauthority         tomd            49    file
.cshrc              tomd           818    file
.exrc               tomd           347    file
.login              tomd           377    file
.mosaic-global      tomd          6988    file
.mosaic-hotlist     tomd            38    file
.mosaic-personal    tomd          1024     dir
.mosaicpid          tomd             5    file
.profile            tomd           382    file
.sh_history         tomd           426    file
.vue                tomd          1024     dir
.vueprofile         tomd          3971    file
700install          tomd        368640    file
Install.mosaic      tomd          6762    file
README.mosaic       tomd          7441    file
README.ninstall     tomd         24354    file
krsort              tomd         34592    file
krsort.c            tomd          3234    file
krsort.dos          tomd         32756    file
krsort.q            tomd          9922    file
krsortorig.c        tomd          3085    file
print.xwd           tomd         44786    file
qsort               tomd         33596    file
qsort.c             tomd          4093    file
qsort.test          tomd          5503    file
qsorttest.q         tomd          4097    file
qsorttest.q         tomd          9081    file
test.xwd            tomd        589291    file

The files listed occupy 1196682 bytes (1.1412 Mbytes)
Average file size is 4738 bytes

$
```

Some trivia to wow your friends with at your next cocktail party: **awk** is the first letter of the last names of its authors: Alfred Aho, Peter Weinberger, and Brian Kernighan.

Chapter 9

HP Visual User Environment

(HP VUE) Introduction

HP VUE

Before I even begin talking about HP VUE, I want to cite other reading material on this and a related topic. HP produces an HP Visual Environment 3.0 User's Guide (part number B1171-90079) which covers HP VUE in careful detail. This user's guide goes well beyond the topics covered in this chapter so you may want to obtain it. Common Desktop Environment (CDE) is another user interface that runs on HP-UX that is based in large part on HP VUE. If you are using CDE you'll want to buy Configuring the Common Desktop Environment by Charlie Fernandez (Prentice Hall, 1995). Charlie is a user interface guru who knows everything about HP VUE and CDE and supplies a wealth of useful CDE information in his book.

You already know something about HP VUE from the "Login and Password" chapter. In that chapter we logged in to a system using the HP VUE login screen. I won't cover that again in this chapter, but will instead focus on the HP VUE environment after you login. I'll introduce you to the most important features of HP VUE. Figure 9-1 is an

HP VUE screen shot showing a typical HP VUE session after a user has logged in.

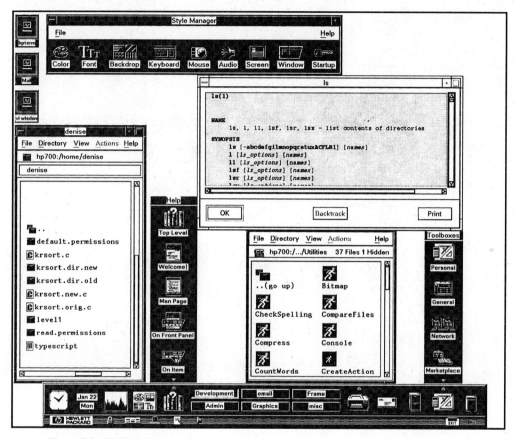

Figure 9-1   HP VUE Screen

We will cover many of the components of HP VUE shown in Figure 9-1 in the following sections. This is a Regular HP VUE session. You can also select an HP VUE Lite Session on your system, which contains a subset of the functionality covered in the following sections. You can select an HP VUE Lite Session from the login screen.

Front Panel

The front panel gives you control over HP VUE components. Figure 9-2 shows an HP VUE front panel.

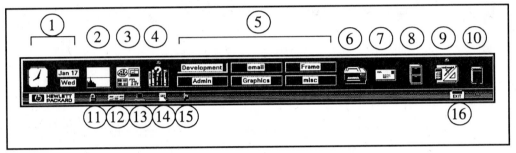

Figure 9-2   HP VUE Front Panel

The items in Figure 9-2 are numbered 1 through 16. Here is a description of each of the items.

1. Clock and Date.

2. Load - Displays activity.

3. Style Manager - Used to change display appearance and behavior. This will be covered in an upcoming section.

4. Help Manager - Slide up subpanel that provides access to all the on line help on your system.

5. Workspaces - Six different workspaces are shown here. These are like different desktops where you can customize each workspace to suit your needs. To switch to another workspace choose the desired workspace from the front panel.

6. Printer - Slide up subpanel with which you can view print status. This is also a drop zone in which file icons can be dropped and printed.

7. Mailer - Starts electronic mail application.

8. File Manager - Starts a file manager window. This will be covered in an upcoming section.

9. Toolbox - Opens toolboxes, including your custom toolbox into which you can add applications. This will be covered in an upcoming section.

10. Trash Can - Put your trash here. Files that are no longer needed can be put in the trash can by dropping an icon onto the trash can.

11. Lock - Locks your display and keyboard, which can only be unlocked with your password.

12. Rename Workspace - Change the names of workspaces, as I have done with the six workspaces shown.

13. Terminal Emulator - Start a terminal emulator so you can enter commands.

14. Text Editor - Starts the HP VUE editor.

15. Audio Button - Control such audio functions as volume, input, and output.

16. Logout - Select this button to log out.

Since HP VUE is easy to use it doesn't make any sense to cover all of its possible functionality. It would be a better use of your time to look at just a few key areas of HP VUE. Let's look further into using the style manager to customize your HP VUE environment, using different workspaces, the file manager, and the general toolbox.

Style Manager

When you select item number 3 from Figure 9-2 you start the style manager. Figure 9-3 shows the style manager. With the style manager you can control the following appearance and behavior aspects of your HP VUE environment:

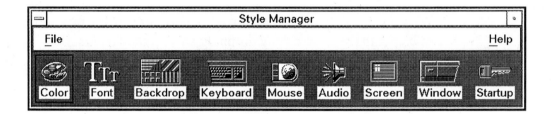

Figure 9-3   Style Manager

Color   Control the color of a workspace. This means that
                 all of your workspaces can have different color
                 characteristics.

Font   Select font sizes.

Backdrop   Select backdrop for workspace. All of your work-
                 spaces can have different backdrops. Figure 9-4
                 shows what happens when you select *Backdrop*
                 from the style manager. A list of available back-
                 drops is produced. You can view a backdrop by
                 selecting it. You can then *Apply* the backdrop to
                 your workspace if you so desire.

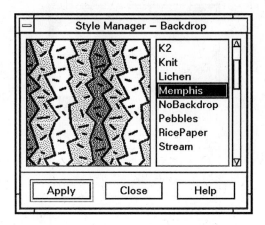

Figure 9-4   Backdrop from Style Manager

Keyboard	Adjust keyboard characteristics.
Mouse	Adjust mouse characteristics.
Audio	Adjust audio characteristics.
Screen	Set screen time out and related characteristics.
Window	Manage window characteristics and icons.
Startup	Manage how your session begins and ends. You have a home session in HP VUE. When you create the setup that you like, you can define that setup as your home session with the button shown in Figure 9-5. You can also control how your next session will begin when you log out. You can select whether you wish to go back to your home session, resume the current session as you have set it up, or be asked each time you log out which session you wish to start at your next login. Figure 9-5 shows the *Startup*.

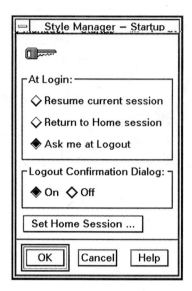

Figure 9-5   Startup from Style Manager

Workspaces

You may find that your needs vary from workspace to workspace. You move between workspaces by selecting the desired workspace from the front panel. As we just covered under the style manager, you can set the color and backdrop in one workspace differently than another. As you switch between your workspaces you will then have each one setup optimally for the applications you use in that workspace. Figure 9-6 shows two different workspaces that have been customized differently. Since the figures are in black and white, you can't see the differences between colors.

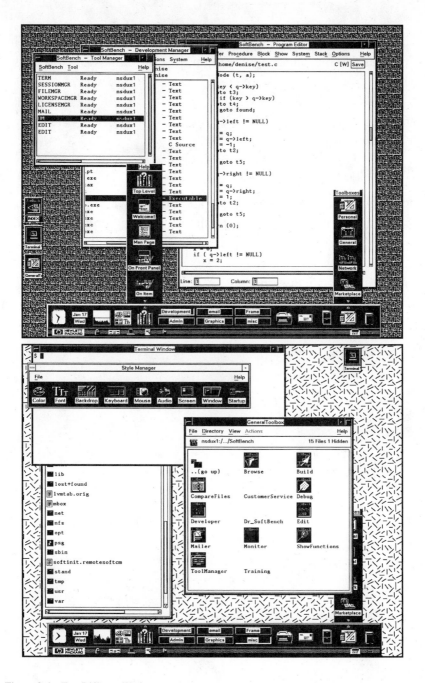

Figure 9-6 Two Different Workspaces

You can see many differences in these two workspaces. This is the same user and the same login session, just different workspaces within HP VUE.

File Manager

The file manager displays each file and directory as an icon. You can move a file to a location, such as the trash can, by dragging the icon to the new location. You can also copy an icon to a location, such as another file manager window, by holding the *Ctrl* key while dragging the icon. Figure 9-7 shows a file manager window. A file is selected and the pull down *File* menu is shown in this figure with some of the file related actions you can perform.

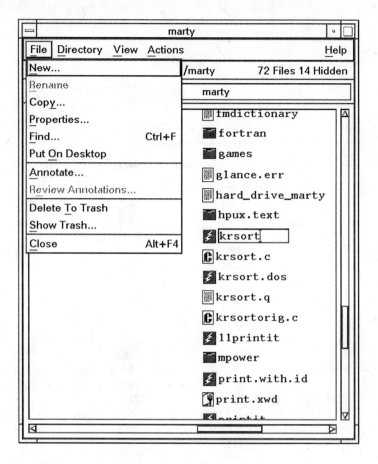

Figure 9-7 File Manager

You can see there are a variety of different icons in the file manager such as source files, executables, directories, and so on. The pull down menu shows some of the file manipulation you can perform in the file manager.

Tool Boxes

You can organize the "tools" you use to get your job done by using the tool-box slide up subpanel. The slide up subpanel itself, from which you can select a toolbox, is shown in the bottom right of Figure 9-1. Among the tool boxes you have are a general and personal toolbox. Figure 9-8 shows part of the general toolbox.

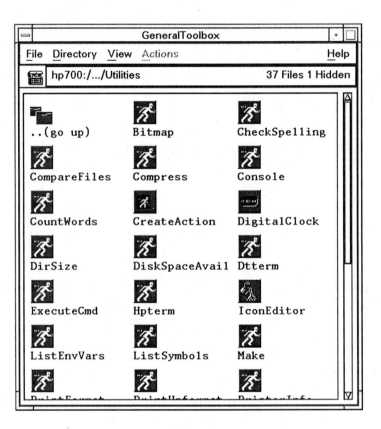

Figure 9-8 General Toolbox

You can see there are all kinds of utilities in the general tool box for getting work done. If you have personal applications you can include these in your personal toolbox to get quick access to them.

Changing Your PATH

You have an environment variable called PATH that determines what directories will be searched when you issue commands. You have many environment variables in the default POSIX shell (see the shell programming chapter) and PATH is one of them. Your system administrator has setup a default PATH for you to use. If you wish to change or add to PATH as an HP VUE user, you would make an entry in the file in your home directory called **.vueprofile**. If you type **env** at the command line, all of your environment variables will be shown. An example of a PATH that was setup on a system I often use looks like the following.

PATH=/opt/softbench/bin:/usr/vue/bin:/usr/bin/X11:/usr/bin:/usr/ccs/bin:
/opt/ansic/bin:usr/contrib/bin:usr/contrib/bin/X11:/opt/upgrade/bin:
/opt/hpnp/bin:/opt/CC/bin:/opt/langtools/bin:/opt/enware/bin:/opt/perf/bin:
/opt/imake/bin:/opt/lrom/bin:/opt/hpxt/enware/bin

If you were to install a new application called "newapp" and wanted to include the directory in which commands associated with the application are located, you could append the directory to your existing PATH. This would be done in your **.vueprofile**. If you look at your existing **.vueprofile** you will probably see mostly comments (lines beginning with #). You could add a line to **.vueprofile** like the following:

```
PATH=$PATH:/opt/newapp/bin
```

/opt/newapp/bin will be appended to the end of the existing PATH in this example. The colon is the delimiter. You could put a colon at the end of **/opt/newapp/bin** and add another name to the PATH. You could substitute any directory you like for **/opt/newapp/bin**.

Adding to Your HP VUE Menu

I covered the toolbox along with many other topics in this chapter. I do not, however, use the toolbox. I want what I want when I want it. I don't like to use the toolbox because I have to go find it. I prefer to put what I need in the pull down menu in my HP VUE environment. This makes for a cluttered menu, but when I hit the right mouse button my menu appears no matter where I am.

It is easy to customize your menu. You need a file in your user area that you can customize called **$HOME/.vue/vuewmrc** where **$HOME** is your home directory. You may not have this file and have to ask your system administrator to give you a copy of it. This file contains a lot of information about your HP VUE environment. By default your menu consists of only one block of commands. You can easily make your menu multitiered by adding submenus. In the following example I have taken the default menu and added two tiers to it. The first is labeled "Root Apps Menu" and the second is labeled "Marty's sys admin scripts." I perform a lot of system administration so I like my scripts handy. Compare the lines under "Vue-RootMenu" in your **.vuewmrc** file to the following customization of **.vuewmrc**.

```
###
#
# Root Menu Description
#
###

Menu VueRootMenu
{
    "Customized Menu"                   f.title
    "Shuffle Up"                        f.circle_up
    "Shuffle Down"                      f.circle_down
    "Refresh"                           f.refresh
    "Minimize/Restore Front Panel"      f.toggle_frontpanel
     no-label                           f.separator
    "Restart Workspace Manager..."      f.restart
     no-label                           f.separator
    "Root Apps Menu"                    f.menu RootAppsMenu
    "Log out..."                        f.action EXIT_SESSION
}
```

```
Menu RootAppsMenu
{
    "SAM"                           f.exec sam
    "LaserROM"                      f.exec lrom
    "Screen Dump"                   f.exec /home/marty/printscreenxpr
    "Window Dump"                   f.exec /home/marty/printwindowxpr
    "Marty's sys admin scripts"     f.menu martyscripts
}
}

Menu martyscripts
{
    "hostck"      f.exec "hpterm -e /home/marty/shell/hostck &"
    "ifstat"      f.exec "hpterm -e /home/marty/shell/ifstat &"
    "gkill"       f.exec "hpterm -e /home/marty/shell/gkill &"
    "llsum"       f.exec "hpterm -e /home/marty/shell/llsum &"
    "psg"         f.exec "hpterm -e /home/marty/shell/psg &"
    "trash"       f.exec "hpterm -e /home/marty/shell/trash &"
    "trash"       f.exec "hpterm -e /home/marty/shell/trash &"
}
```

Let's now see what this menu looks like in Figure 9-9.

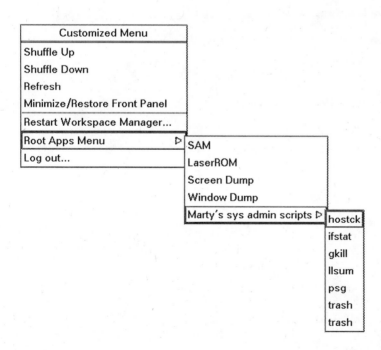

Figure 9-9   Customized HP VUE Menu

This three tier menu provides me with my most often used commands. If you think this might work for you go ahead and update your menu.

Adding to the Front Panel

We covered the layout of the front panel earlier. You can modify or add to the front panel with the **$HOME/.vue/vuewmrc** file.

By default you probably have a top and bottom definition for the front panel. These are definitions for what elements appear in the top and bottom rows of the front panel. The following are definitions in my **vuewmrc** file:

```
################################################################
#
#   Start Front Panel Description: Regular Session
#
################################################################
PANEL FrontPanel
{
   BOX              Top
   BOX              Bottom
}

################################################################
#
#   Regular Session:   Top Row
#
#   The top row is a primary row, containing subpanels and large icons.
#
#   Controls are listed in order, from left to right, and are defined
#   immediately after the "BOX Bottom" block.
#
###
BOX Top
{
   TYPE             primary
   CONTROL          Clock
   CONTROL          Date
   CONTROL          Load
   CONTROL          Style
   CONTROL          Help
   SWITCH           Switch
```

```
            CONTROL           Printer
            CONTROL           Mail
            CONTROL           Home
            CONTROL           Toolboxes
            CONTROL           Trash
            HELP_TOPIC        FPTop
}

###############################################################
#
#  Regular Session:  Bottom Row
#
#   The bottom row is a secondary row.
#
###
BOX Bottom
{
   TYPE              secondary
   CONTROL           Logo
   CONTROL           Lock
   CONTROL           Rename
   CONTROL           Terminal
   CONTROL           XTerminal
   CONTROL           TextEdit
   CONTROL           Busy
   HELP_TOPIC        FPBottom
}
```

If you compare the front panel elements described in your **vuewmrc** with those described in my **vuewmrc,** you may find that you do not have "XTerminal" in your bottom row. This is an element I have added to the bottom row of my front panel.

The following are descriptions of the bottom row controls including the XTerminal I have added.

```
###############################################################
#
#  Regular Session:  Bottom Row Controls
#
###

# Control description:  Logo
#
CONTROL Logo
{
   TYPE              button
```

```
  IMAGE                 logo
  PUSH_ACTION           f.version
  HELP_TOPIC            FPLogo
}

# Control description:  Lock
#
CONTROL Lock
{
  TYPE                  button
  IMAGE                 lock
  PUSH_ACTION           f.action LOCK_DISPLAY
  HELP_TOPIC            FPLock
}

# Control description:  Rename
#
CONTROL Rename
{
  TYPE                  button
  IMAGE                 wsrenam
  PUSH_ACTION           f.workspace_rename
  HELP_TOPIC            FPRename
}

# Control description:  Terminal
#
CONTROL Terminal
{
  TYPE                  button
  IMAGE                 term
  TITLE                 "Terminal_Window"
  PUSH_ACTION           f.action TERMINAL
  HELP_TOPIC            FPTerminal
}

# Control description:  Terminal
#
CONTROL XTerminal
{
  TYPE                  button
  IMAGE                 /usr/vue/icons/termX.1.bm
  TITLE                 "Terminal_Window"
  PUSH_ACTION           f.exec "/usr/bin/X11/xterm -sb -sl 500"
  HELP_TOPIC            FPTerminal
}

# Control description:  TextEdit
#
CONTROL TextEdit
{
  TYPE                  button
  IMAGE                 vuepad
  DROP_ACTION           f.action EditText
  PUSH_ACTION           f.action EditText
  HELP_TOPIC            FPTextEdit
}
```

```
# Control description:  Busy
#
CONTROL Busy
{
  TYPE              busy
  IMAGE             exit
  ALTERNATE_IMAGE   exit02
# LABEL              "Exit"
  PUSH_ACTION       f.action EXIT_SESSION
  HELP_TOPIC        FPBusy
}
###########  End Front Panel Description: Regular Session #######
```

The description of the XTerminal consists of several elements. The *TYPE* is a *button* that you can select. The *IMAGE* is a bitmap that is a file. You can design your own bitmaps or use an existing bitmap. There is a *TITLE* and *PUSH_ACTION*, which I have defined. The *PUSH_ACTION* is the specific command I want issued when the *button* is pushed, which is the **xterm** command with associated options. You can also define your own *HELP_TOPIC* or use existing help.

I have only touched on a few types of customization you can perform in HP VUE. There are a variety of other types of customization possible. You can see the HP VUE users manual or Charlie Fernandez's CDE book for much more detail on this subject.

Chapter 10

The vi Editor

The vi Editor

As you already know from the HP Visual User Environment (HP VUE) chapter, there is a graphical editor supplied with HP VUE. We are now going to take a step back and cover the visual editor, **vi**, which is used to edit text files. With a fine graphics based editor as a standard part of the HP-UX operating system and a plethora of editors available as part of personal computer windowing environments, why are we covering **vi**? The answer is twofold. First, not everyone using HP-UX has access to a graphics display and may therefore need to know and use **vi**. Since **vi** comes with HP-UX and is a powerful editor, many new HP-UX users end up using and liking it. Second, **vi** has traditionally been thought of as *the* UNIX editor. There are few UNIX users who have not used **vi**. This does not mean it is everyone's primary editor; however, virtually all UNIX users have had some experience with **vi**.

I'll cover the basics of using **vi** in this chapter. You can experiment with what is covered here, and if you really like it you can investigate some of the more advanced features of **vi**.

Starting a vi Session

Let's jump right in and edit a file. From the command line we type **vi** and the name of the file we wish to edit, in this case **wisdom**.

```
$ vi wisdom
```

We are then editing the file **wisdom** as shown in Figure 10-1. **wisdom** contains a passage from <u>Tao Te Ching</u> or "Book of the Way." We will use this file throughout this chapter.

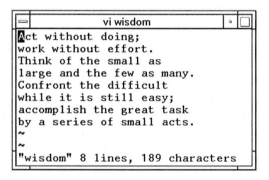

Figure 10-1   Editing the File **wisdom**

The bottom line in Figure 10-1 is the message line in **vi**. After invoking **vi,** the message line indicates the name of the file, the number of lines, and the number of characters in the file. Different messages appear on the message line depending on the command you issue, as we will see in upcoming examples. If a tilde appears on any lines in the file, as it does in the two lines above the message line in **wisdom**, it means there are not enough lines to fill up the screen. The cursor is the dark box that appears at line 1 in Figure 10-1.

We can specify several file names and after saving the first file move on to the second file by entering **:n,** and continue going through the list of files in this way. Or, we can specify a file and position the cursor on the last line in the file. The default is for the cursor to appear over the first character in the file as shown in Figure 10-1.

Table 10-1 shows some of the ways we can start a **vi** session.

Table 10-1 Starting a **vi** Session

Command	Description
vi file	Edit **file.**
vi -r file	Edit last saved version of **file** after a crash.
vi -R file	Edit the file in read only mode.
vi + file	Edit **file** and place cursor on last line.
vi file1 file2 file3 ...	Edit **file1** through **file3** and after saving changes in **file1** you can move to **file2** by entering **:n.**

A feature of **vi** that often confuses new users is that there are modes to **vi**. When you are in *command mode*, everything you type is interpreted as a command. In *command mode* you can specify such actions as the location to which you want the cursor to move. When you are in *input mode,* everything you type is information to be added to the file. *Command mode* is the default when you start **vi**. You can move into *command mode* from *input mode* at any time by hitting the *escape* key. You move into *insert mode* from *command mode* by typing one of the *input mode* commands covered shortly.

Cursor Control Commands

A key skill to develop in **vi** is getting the cursor to the desired position. You do this in *command mode*. There are a variety of ways to move the cursor around the screen. Table 10-2 summarizes some of the more commonly used cursor movements.

Table 10-2 Cursor Control Commands in **vi**

Command	Cursor Movement
h	Move left one character.
j	Move down one line.
k	Move up one line.
l or space	Move right one character.
G	Go to the last line of the file.
nG	Go to line number **n**.
G$	Go to the last character in the file.
w	Go to the beginning of the next word.
b	Go to the beginning of the previous word.
L	Go to the last line of the screen.
M	Go to the middle line of the screen.
H	Go to the first line of the screen.
e	Move to the end word.
(	Go to the beginning of the sentence.
)	Go to the end of the sentence.
{	Go to the beginning of the paragraph.
}	Go to the beginning of the next paragraph.

I know it seems a little strange at first that you have to remember these commands in order to get the cursor to the desired position, but this is the way **vi** works. Let's use w**isdom** to show how some of these cursor movements work. Figures 10-2 and 10-3 show some cursor movements. Like all of the upcoming figures, Figures 10-2 and 10-3 show **wisdom** before a command is entered on the left and the result after the command is entered on the right. The command issued appears in the middle. Some of the commands in upcoming figures use the *enter* and *escape* keys.

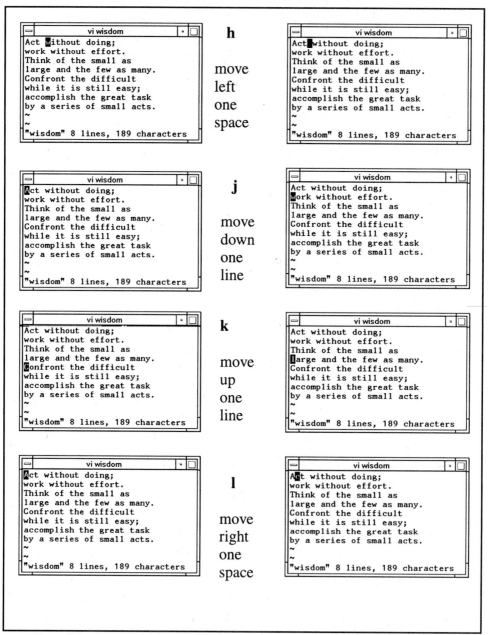

Figure 10-2   Examples of Cursor Movement in **vi** (**h**, **j**, **k**, and **l**)

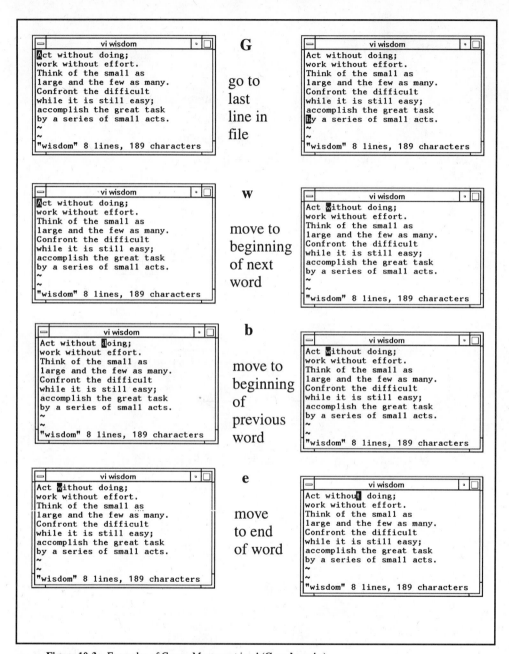

Figure 10-3   Examples of Cursor Movement in **vi** (**G**, **w**, **b**, and **e**)

Adding Text in vi

Now that we know how to move around the cursor, let's do something with it. It is important to first learn about cursor movement since the commands for adding text take place relative to the position of the cursor. Table 10-3 summarizes some commands for adding text.

Table 10-3 Adding Text in **vi**

Command	Insertion Action
a	Append new text after the cursor.
i	Insert new text before the cursor.
o	Open a line below the current line.
O	Open a line above the current line.
:r file	Read file and insert after current line.
escape	Get back to command mode.

Let's now look at some examples for adding text into **wisdom** in Figure 10-4.

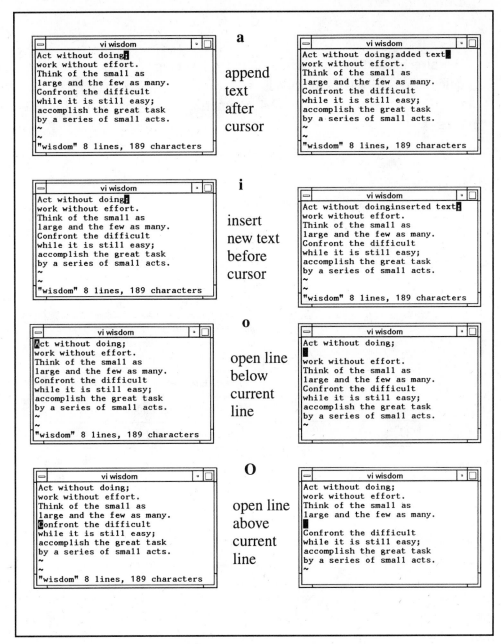

Figure 10-4 Examples of Adding Text in **vi**

Deleting Text in vi

We also needed to learn about cursor movement before learning how to delete text, since the commands for deleting text take place relative to the position of the cursor. Table 10-4 summarizes some commands for deleting text.

Table 10-4 Deleting Text in **vi**

Command	Deletion Action
x	Delete the character at the cursor. You can also put a number in front of x to specify the number of characters to delete.
X	Delete the previous character. You can also put a number in front of X to specify the number of previous characters to delete.
dw	Delete to the beginning of the next word.
dG	Delete lines to the end of the file.
dd	Delete the entire line.
db	Delete the previous word. You can also put a number in front of db to specify the number of previous words to delete.

Let's now look at some examples for deleting text from **wisdom** in Figures 10-5 and 10-6.

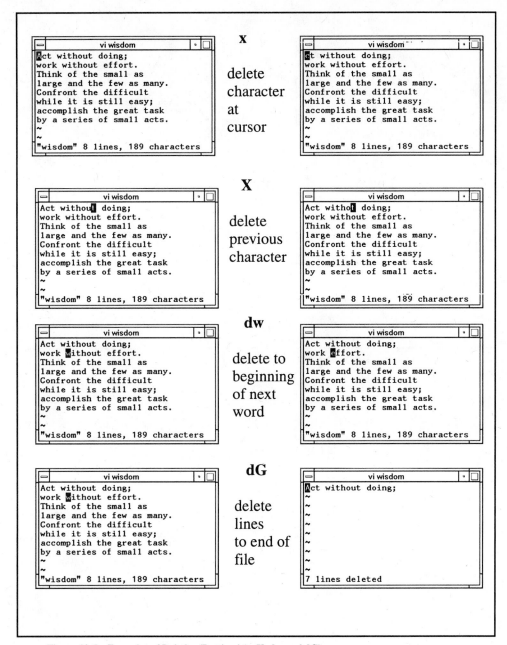

Figure 10-5 Examples of Deleting Text in **vi** (**x**, **X**, **dw**, and **dG**)

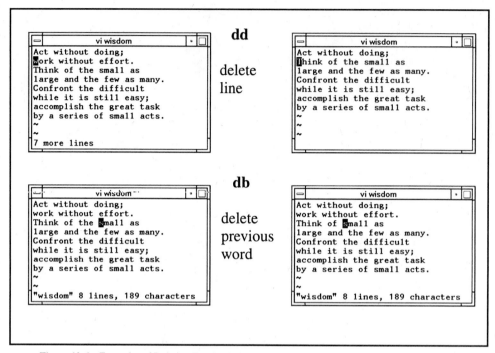

Figure 10-6   Examples of Deleting Text in **vi** (**dd** and **db**)

Changing Text in vi

Okay, you've added text, deleted text, now you want to change text. **vi** isn't so bad so far, is it? Table 10-5 summarizes some commands for changing text.

Table 10-5 Changing Text in **vi**

Command (Preceding these commands with a number repeats the commands any number of times.)	**Replacement Action**
rX	Replace the current character with **X**.
R	Replace the current characters until *escape* is entered.
cw	Change to the beginning of the next word.
cG	Change to the end of the file.
cc	Change the entire line.

Let's now look at some examples of replacing text from **wisdom** in Figures 10-7 and 10-8.

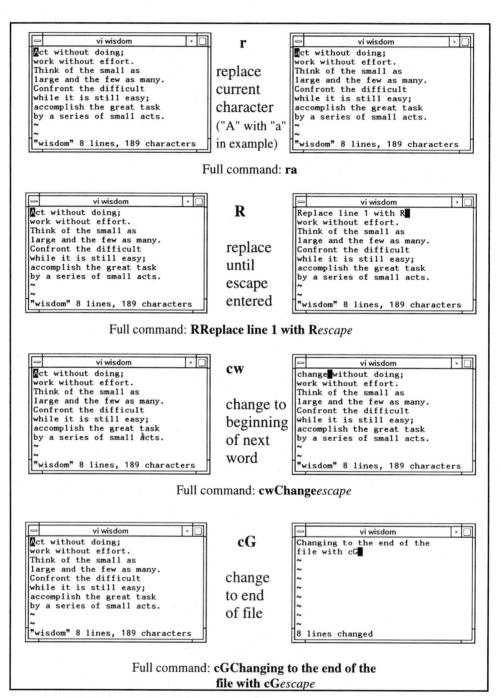

Figure 10-7   Examples of Changing Text in **vi** (**r**, **R**, **cw**, **cG**)

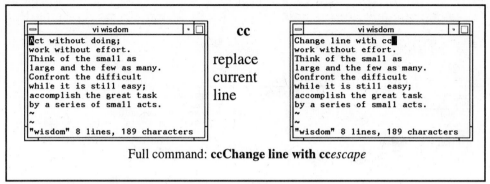

Full command: **ccChange line with cc***escape*

Figure 10-8 Example of Changing Text in **vi** with **cc**

Search and Replace in vi

You have a lot of search and replace functionality in **vi**. Table 10-6 summarizes some of the more common search and replace functionality in **vi**.

Table 10-6 Search and Replace in **vi**

Command	Search and Replace Action
/text	Search for **text** going forward into the file.
?text	Search for **text** going backward into the file.
n	Repeat search in the same direction as the original search.
N	Repeat the search in the opposite direction as the original search.
:s/oldtext/newtext/	Substitute **newtext** for **oldtext**.
:m,ns/oldtext/newtext/	Substitute **newtext** for **oldtext** in lines **m** through **n**.

Let's now look at some examples of searching and replacing text in **wisdom** in Figure 10-9.

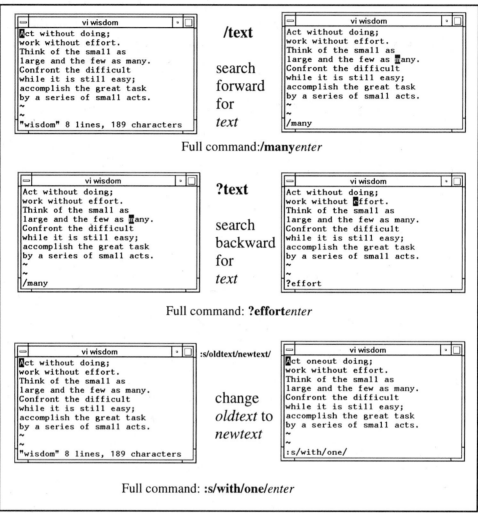

Figure 10-9   Examples of Search and Replace in **vi**

Copying Text in vi

You can copy text in **vi**. Some commands for copying are shown in Table 10-7.

Table 10-7 Copying in **vi**

Command	Copy Action
yy	Yank the current line.
nyy	Yank **n** lines.
p (lower case)	Put yanked text after cursor.
p (upper case)	Put yanked text before cursor.

Let's now look at some examples of copying text in **wisdom** in Figure 10-10.

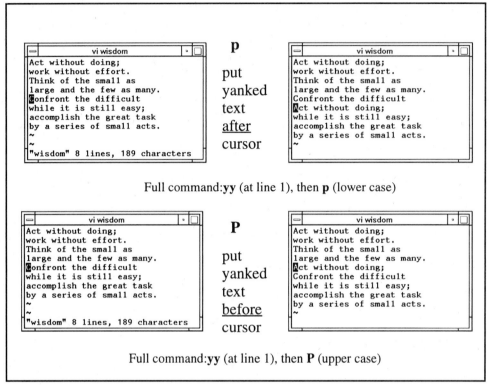

Figure 10-10   Copying in **vi**

Undo in vi

You can easily undo changes in **vi** with the commands shown in Table 10-8.

Table 10-8 Undo in **vi**

Command	Undo Action
u	Undo the last change.
U	Undo all changes to the current line.

Table 10-8 Undo in **vi**

Command	Undo Action
. (period)	Repeat the last change.

Save Text and Exit vi

There are a number of different ways to save files and exit **vi**, some of which are summarized in Table 10-9.

Table 10-9 Saving Text and Exiting **vi**

Command	Save and/or Quit Action
:w	Save the file but don't exit **vi**.
:w filename	Save changes in the file **filename** but don't quit **vi**.
:wq	Save the file and quit **vi**.
:q!	Quit **vi** without saving the file.

Options in vi

There are many options you can set and unset in **vi**. To set an option you type **:set** *option.* To unset an option you type **:set no***option.* Table 10-10 summarizes some of the more commonly used options.

Table 10-10 vi Options

Option	Action
:set all	Print all options.
:set no*option*	Turn off ***option***.
:set nu	Prefix lines with line number.
:set ro	Set file to read only.
:set showmode	Show whether input or replace mode.
:set warn	Print a warning message if there has not been a write since the last change to the file.

Let's now look at some examples of replacing text from **wisdom** in Figure 10-11.

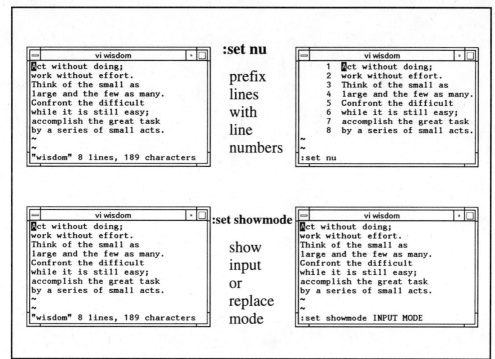

Figure 10-11   Options in **vi**

Chapter 11

HP-UX System Administration Introduction

System Administration Introduction

First, let me say in no uncertain terms that I have no intention of doing justice to HP-UX system administration in one chapter. This simply can't be done. I do, however, have the following objectives for this chapter:

1) Recap some of the topics related to system administration covered in previous chapters.

2) Cover some system administration tasks that you may be given the opportunity to perform. For instance, both you and your system administrator may agree that you have a need to start backups, load software, or perform other system administration tasks. I'll cover what I believe to be some

of the more common system administration topics that users sometimes end up learning about.

System Administration Topics Already Covered

We have already covered some of the most important system administration topics in previous chapters. These include: the HP-UX file system; HP-UX networking; HP Visual User Environment (HP VUE); and shell programming. These are areas where system administrators spend a great deal of their time.

Managing the HP-UX file system can be nearly a full-time job for system administrators. Organizing logical volumes and managing these consumes a lot of time and requires an extensive knowledge of logical volume manager. As a user, however, you should have to spend a minimal amount of time on logical volumes. This is the responsibility of your system administrator.

HP-UX networking is also an area that requires knowledge of specialized networking commands. The chapter I devoted to HP-UX networking is fairly complete, so I won't provide any additional networking background.

I also covered HP VUE and shell programming in detail in previous chapters, so there isn't much more to cover in this chapter.

The other areas of system administration I find users sometimes need to know about are the System Administration Manager (SAM) and Software Distributor-HP-UX for loading software. I will cover these two topics in this chapter.

System Administration Manager (SAM)

You may be given restricted access to the System Administrator Manager (SAM) so you can perform various system administration tasks. You can perform all kinds of tasks with SAM that users sometimes like to handle themselves, such as starting your own backup and managing a local printer. Beginning with HP-UX 10.x your system administrator can set up restricted access to some SAM functional areas for you. It may be, for instance, that your system administrator thinks you should be able to start a backup of your user area. He or she can give you access to this area of SAM.

Here are the major headings under the SAM main menu:

- Accounts for Users and Groups

- Auditing and Security

- Backup and Recovery

- Disks and File Systems

- Kernel Configuration

- Networking and Communications

- Peripheral Devices

- Printers and Plotters

- Process Management

- Routine Tasks

- Run SAM on Remote Systems

- Software Management

- Time

Figure 11-1 shows the graphical user interface of SAM, through which you could select any of the functional areas to which your system administrator gives you access.

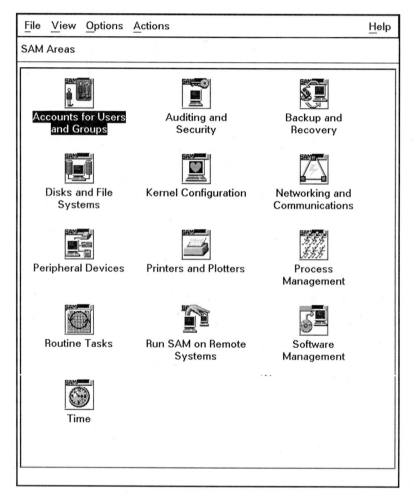

Figure 11-1 SAM Startup Window in Graphics Mode

In addition to selecting a functional area you can select from the pull-down menu bar across the top of the SAM window. I will indicate selections made in SAM and keyboard keys in this chapter with italics. The five selections are *File, View, Options, Actions,* and *Help.* The title line shown in the figure reads *SAM Areas*. If you're running Restricted SAM Builder you will also see a status line with the message "Privileges for user: <user-name>". If your system administrator gives you restricted access you will see your user name. As you progress down the hierarchy the title line will change to reflect your level in the SAM hierarchy. You can move into one of the areas shown, such as *Backup and Recovery*, by double clicking the left mouse button on this functional area. You move back up the hierarchy by selecting the *Actions-Close Level* menu pick.

You don't need a graphics display to run SAM. You have access to nearly all the same functionality on a text terminal as you do on a graphics terminal. Figure 11-2 is SAM running in character mode with the same 13 functional areas you have in graphics mode.

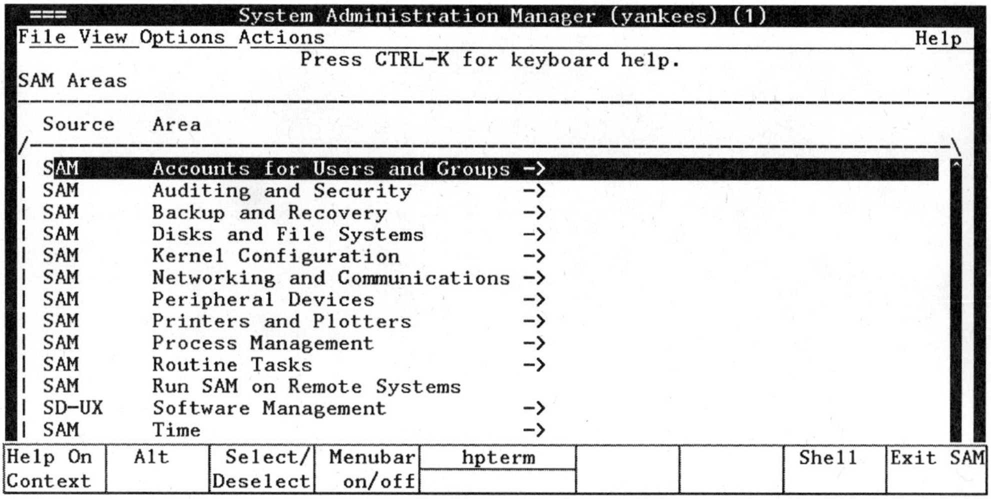

```
 ===              System Administration Manager (yankees) (1)
File View Options Actions                                              Help
                      Press CTRL-K for keyboard help.
SAM Areas
------------------------------------------------------------------------------
    Source     Area
/-----------------------------------------------------------------------------\
|  SAM       Accounts for Users and Groups ->                               |^|
|  SAM       Auditing and Security          ->                              | |
|  SAM       Backup and Recovery            ->                              | |
|  SAM       Disks and File Systems         ->                              | |
|  SAM       Kernel Configuration           ->                              | |
|  SAM       Networking and Communications  ->                             | |
|  SAM       Peripheral Devices             ->                              | |
|  SAM       Printers and Plotters          ->                              | |
|  SAM       Process Management             ->                              | |
|  SAM       Routine Tasks                  ->                              | |
|  SAM       Run SAM on Remote Systems                                      | |
|  SD-UX     Software Management            ->                              | |
|  SAM       Time                           ->                              | |
------------------------------------------------------------------------------
Help On | Alt   | Select/| Menubar|   hpterm      |       |     | Shell |Exit SAM
Context |       |Deselect| on/off |               |       |     |       |
```

Figure 11-2   SAM Start Up Window in Character Mode

The View menu can be used in character mode to tailor the information desired, filter out some entries, or search for particular entries. Because you don't have a mouse on a text terminal, you use the keyboard to make selections. The point and click method of using SAM when in graphics mode is highly preferable to using the keyboard; however, the same structure to the functional areas exists in both environments. When you see an item in reverse video on the text terminal (such as *Accounts For Users and Groups* in Figure 11-2), you know you have that item selected. After having selected *Accounts For Users and Groups* as shown in the Figure 11-2, you would then use the *tab* key (or *F4*) to get to the menu bar, use the <- -> keys to select the desired menu, and use the *space bar* to display the menu. This is where having a mouse to make your selections is highly desirable. Figure 11-3 shows a menu bar selection for both a text and graphics display. In both cases the *Actions* menu of *Disks and File Systems* has been selected.

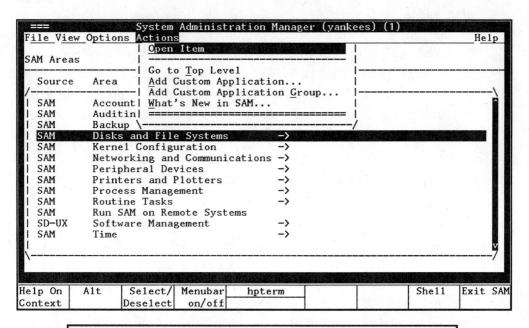

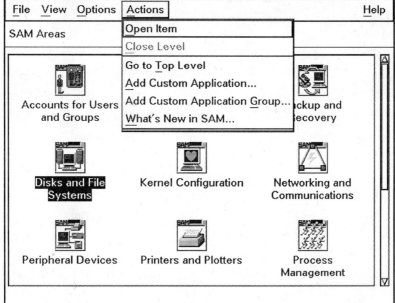

Figure 11-3 SAM Menu Selection for Text and Graphics Displays

Of particular interest on the pull down menu are *Add Custom Application* and *Add Custom Application Group*. This means that your system administrator can customize SAM to meet your specific administration needs by adding functionality to SAM. An application to perform most any application can be added to SAM in this way. It is, however, the prerogative of your system administrator to add, or decline to add, functionality to SAM. But now that you know it exists, you can request that you be given access to the functionality you think you need, if it will not jeopardize other users of your system.

Installing Software with Software Distributor-HP-UX

You may be given the ability to load software on your system by your system administrator. Beginning with HP-UX 10.x you would use Software Distributor-HP-UX (typically called SD-UX or Software Distributor) to load software.

Software Distributor is a standards-based way to perform software management. It conforms to the Portable Operating System Interface (POSIX) standard for packaging software and utilities related to software management. The Software Distributor product described in this section comes with your HP-UX system. There is additional functionality you can obtain by buying the OpenView Software Distributor (SD-OV) product. SD-OV provides support for additional platforms and allows you to "push" software out to target systems. In this section I won't cover SD-OV, but will make some comments about SD-OV functionality where appropriate.

Software Distributor can be invoked using the commands described in this section, by using SAM, which was just covered, or by installing software for the first time.

The following are the four phases of software installation performed with Software Distributor:

- Selection - You can select the source and software you wish to load during this phase. In the upcoming example the graphical user interface of Software Distributor is used and you'll see how easy it is to select the source and software. With SD-OV you could also select the target on which you wish to load software - remember the SD-OV "push" capability?

- Analysis- All kinds of checks are performed for you, including free disk space; dependencies; compatibility; mounted volumes; and others. Among the very useful outputs of this phase is the amount of space the software you wish to load will consume on each logical volume. This will be shown in the example.

- Load - After you are satisfied with the analysis, you may proceed with loading the software.

- Configuration - It is possible the software you load requires kernel rebuilding and a system reboot. Start up and shutdown scripts may also need to be modified.

There is some terminology associated with Software Distributor that I tend to use somewhat loosely. I have nothing but good things to say about Software Distributor, but I don't tend to conform to the official Software Distributor terminology as much as I should. I tend, for instance, to use the word system a lot, which could mean many different things in the Software Distributor world. For instance, Software Distributor uses local host (a system on which Software Distributor is running or software is to be installed or managed by Software Distributor), distribution depot (a directory which is used as a place for software products), and development system (a place where software is prepared for distribution). I will use the word system to mean the system on which we are working in the examples, because software is loaded onto the system from CD-ROM.

Software Distributor Tasks

Here are some of the common software management related tasks you can perform with Software Distributor:

Installing and Updating Software (command line or GUI)

The **swinstall** command is used to install and update software. The source of the software you are loading can come from a variety of places including CD-ROM, magnetic tape, or a "depot" directory from which software can be distributed. Using the depot, you can load software into a directory and then install and update software on other nodes from this directory. Software loaded from CD-ROM with Software Distributor must be loaded onto the local system; this technique is used in the upcoming example. You have a lot of flexibility with SD-OV only when selecting the target system onto which you want to load software and the source from which you will load the software. You can, for instance, load software from a depot which is on another system on your network. This command can be run at the command line or with the graphical user interface.

Copying Software to a Depot (command line or GUI)

The **swcopy** command is used to copy software from one depot to another. The depot used in the upcoming examples is a CD-ROM. By setting up depots, you can quickly install or update software to other nodes simultaneously with SD-OV only. This command can be run at the command line or with the graphical user interface.

Removing Software From A System (command line or GUI)

The **swremove** command is used to remove software from a system that has had software loaded with Software Distributor. This includes removing installed and configured software from a system or removing software from a depot. This command can be run at the command line or with the graphical user interface.

List Information about Installation Software

The **swlist** command provides information about the depots that exist on a system, the contents of a depot, or information about installed software. Examples of using this command are provided shortly.

Configure Installed Software

The **swconfig** command configures or unconfigures installed software. Configuration of software normally takes place as part of **swinstall** but configuration can be deferred until a later time.

Verify Software

The **swverify** command confirms the integrity of installed software or software stored in a depot.

Package Software That Can Later Be Installed (local system only)

You may want to produce "packages" of software that you can later put on tape or in a depot with the **swpackage** command. This packaged software can then be used as a source for **swinstall** and be managed by other Software Distributor commands.

Control Access to Software Distributor Objects

You may want to apply restricted access to Software Distributor objects such as packaged software. Using the **swacl** command, you can view and change the Access Control List (ACL) for objects.

Modify Information about Loaded Software (local system only)

The Installed Products Database (IPD) and associated files are used to maintain information about software products you have loaded. **swmodify** can be run at the command line to modify these files.

Register Or Unregister a Depot

A software depot can be registered or unregistered with **swreg**. This means you don't have to remove a depot if you temporarily don't want it used, you can unregister it.

Manage Jobs (command line or GUI, this is SD-OV only)

Software Distributor jobs can be viewed and removed with **swjob**. The graphical user interface version of this command can be invoked with **sd** or **swjob -i**.

Software Distributor Example

The example of Software Distributor in this section describes the process of loading software from CD-ROM to the local system. What I'll show here only begins to scratch the surface of functionality you have with Software Distributor, but, since I want to give you only an overview this should be sufficient. You can load software from a variety of media as well as across the network. The graphical user interface that appears throughout this section makes the process of dealing with software easy. You don't, however, have to use this graphical user interface. You can use the **swinstall** command from the command line specifying source, options, target, and so on. I would recommend using the graphical user interface because this is so much easier. If, however, you like to do things the "traditional UNIX" way, you can issue the **swinstall** command with arguments. You can look at the manual page for **swinstall** to understand its arguments and options and use this command from the command line. The graphical user interface of Software Distributor works with many Software Distributor commands, including **sd** (this is an SD-OV command and may also be invoked with **swjob -i**), **swcopy**, **swremove**, and **swinstall**. There is also an interactive terminal user interface for these commands if you don't have a graphics display.

The first step when loading software from CD-ROM is to insert the media and mount the CD-ROM. The directory **/SD_CDROM** should already exist on your HP-UX 10.x system. If not, you can create this directory or use any name you like. You can use SAM to mount the CD-ROM for you or do this manually. I issued the following commands to mount a CD-ROM at SCSI address two on a workstation and start Software Distributor:

```
$ mount /dev/dsk/c0t2d0 /SD_CDROM

$ swinstall
```

Software Distributor may look for a software depot on your local system as a default source location for software. If this is not found you'll
receive a dialog box in which you can change the source depot path. In this
case I changed the source depot path to the default for a CD-ROM, /
SD_CDROM. This is the Selection process described earlier whereby you
select the source and target for software to be loaded. You can now select
the specific software you wish to load.

When the *Software Selection* Window is opened for you, you can perform many different operations. To identify software bundles you wish to
load on your system, you can highlight these and *Mark For Install* from the
Actions menu as I have done in Figure 11-4 for <u>The C/ANSI C Developers
Bundle</u>.

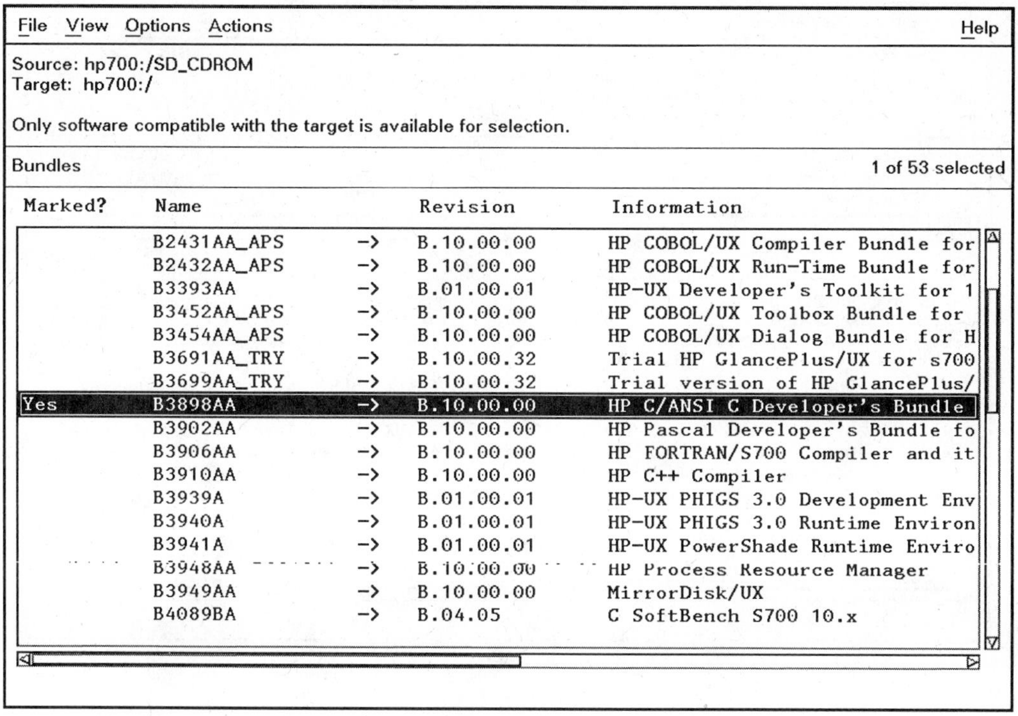

```
 ┌─────────────────────────────────────────────────────────────────────────────┐
 │  File  View  Options  Actions                                          Help   │
 ├─────────────────────────────────────────────────────────────────────────────┤
 │  Source: hp700:/SD_CDROM                                                      │
 │  Target:  hp700:/                                                             │
 │                                                                               │
 │  Only software compatible with the target is available for selection.         │
 ├─────────────────────────────────────────────────────────────────────────────┤
 │  Bundles                                                      1 of 53 selected │
 ├─────────────────────────────────────────────────────────────────────────────┤
 │  ┌─────────────────────────────────────────────────────────────────────────┐ │
 │  │ Marked?    Name                   Revision        Information           │ │
 │  ├─────────────────────────────────────────────────────────────────────────┤ │
 │  │            B2431AA_APS    ->   B.10.00.00   HP COBOL/UX Compiler Bundle for ▲ │
 │  │            B2432AA_APS    ->   B.10.00.00   HP COBOL/UX Run-Time Bundle for   │
 │  │            B3393AA        ->   B.01.00.01   HP-UX Developer's Toolkit for 1   │
 │  │            B3452AA_APS    ->   B.10.00.00   HP COBOL/UX Toolbox Bundle for    │
 │  │            B3454AA_APS    ->   B.10.00.00   HP COBOL/UX Dialog Bundle for H   │
 │  │            B3691AA_TRY    ->   B.10.00.32   Trial HP GlancePlus/UX for s700   │
 │  │            B3699AA_TRY    ->   B.10.00.32   Trial version of HP GlancePlus/   │
 │  │ █Yes       B3898AA        ->   B.10.00.00   HP C/ANSI C Developer's Bundle █  │
 │  │            B3902AA        ->   B.10.00.00   HP Pascal Developer's Bundle fo   │
 │  │            B3906AA        ->   B.10.00.00   HP FORTRAN/S700 Compiler and it   │
 │  │            B3910AA        ->   B.10.00.00   HP C++ Compiler                   │
 │  │            B3939A         ->   B.01.00.01   HP-UX PHIGS 3.0 Development Env    │
 │  │            B3940A         ->   B.01.00.01   HP-UX PHIGS 3.0 Runtime Environ   │
 │  │            B3941A         ->   B.01.00.01   HP-UX PowerShade Runtime Enviro   │
 │  │            B3948AA        ->   B.10.00.00   HP Process Resource Manager       │
 │  │            B3949AA        ->   B.10.00.00   MirrorDisk/UX                     │
 │  │            B4089BA        ->   B.04.05      C SoftBench S700 10.x           ▼ │
 │  └─────────────────────────────────────────────────────────────────────────┘ │
 │  ◁                                                                          ▷ │
 └─────────────────────────────────────────────────────────────────────────────┘
```

Figure 11-4   Software Distributor *Software Selection* Window

A bundle, such as the one selected, may be comprised of products, subproducts, and filesets. You can select *Open Item* from the *Actions* menu if you want to drop down one level to see the subproducts or filesets. Figure 11-5 shows *Open Item* for C/ANSI C Developers Bundle.

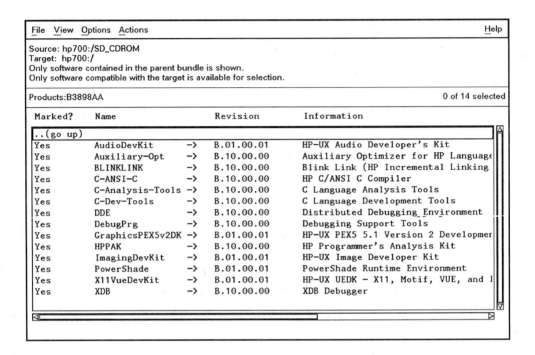

Figure 11-5   Software Distributor *Open Item*

After you have specified items to *Mark For Install,* you can select *Install (analysis)* from the *Actions* menu. Before starting analysis or before loading software you should select *Show Description Of Software* from the *Actions* menu to see if a system reboot is required (you may have to scroll down the window to see the bottom of the description). You want to know this before you load software so you don't load software that requires a reboot at a time that it is inconvenient to reboot. Figure 11-6 is an example *Install Analysis* window for installing Trail HP GlancePlus/UX for s700.

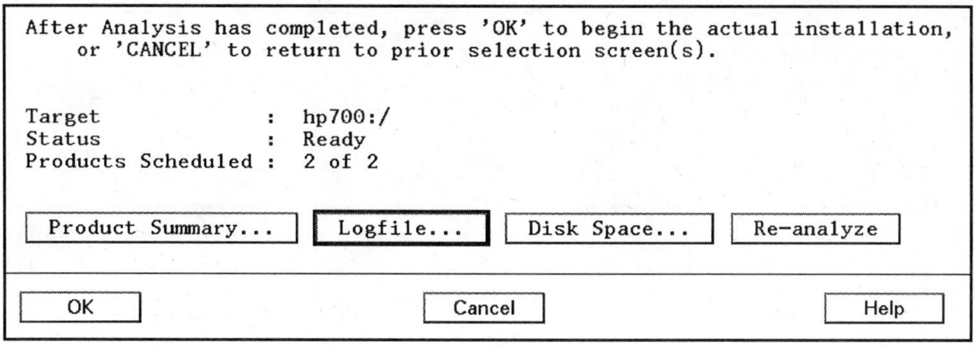

```
After Analysis has completed, press 'OK' to begin the actual installation,
   or 'CANCEL' to return to prior selection screen(s).


Target              :   hp700:/
Status              :   Ready
Products Scheduled  :   2 of 2


 ┌─────────────────────┐  ┌─────────────────┐  ┌─────────────────┐  ┌─────────────────┐
 │  Product Summary... │  │  Logfile...     │  │  Disk Space...  │  │  Re-analyze     │
 └─────────────────────┘  └─────────────────┘  └─────────────────┘  └─────────────────┘

 ┌──────────┐               ┌──────────────┐                        ┌──────────────┐
 │   OK     │               │   Cancel     │                        │    Help      │
 └──────────┘               └──────────────┘                        └──────────────┘
```

Figure 11-6   Software Distributor *Install Analysis* Window

You can see that there are two products to be loaded in this bundle. Among the many useful pieces of information the analysis window provides you is a *Logfile* that contains a good review of the analysis, and a *Disk Space* window that shows the amount of space that will be consumed by the software you plan to load. Figure 11-7 shows the *Disk Space* window, which includes the amount of disk space available on the affected Logical Volumes both before and after the software load takes place.

File View Options Actions		Help

Target: hp700:/   Sizes shown in Kbytes.
All affected file systems on hp700:/ are listed.
To view software affecting a filesystem, open the filesystem.

File Systems   0 of 4 selected

File System Mount Point		Available Before	Available After	Capacity After	Must Free
/	->	23240	23210	51%	0
/opt	->	57858	51116	48%	0
/usr	->	119551	119548	60%	0
/var	->	26021	25994	24%	0

Figure 11-7   Software Distributor *Disk Space* from Analysis

This window is a dream come true for system administrators who have traditionally not had a lot of good information about either the amount of space consumed by the software they are loading or the destination of the software they are loading. You also have menus here that allow you to further investigate the software you're about to load on your system.

After you are satisfied with the analysis information, you may proceed with loading the software.

Chapter 12

Programming With SoftBench

Getting Started

If you are going to be programming as a new HP-UX user, as opposed to using an existing off the shelf application, you have many options for your programming environment. Among your many options are the standard HP-UX programming tools, many third party applications, and HP SoftBench. Because so many new users with whom I work use the HP SoftBench environment, I decided to include this chapter.

HP's SoftBench application development environment includes a comprehensive set of integrated, easy-to-use, program construction tools for C, C++, and COBOL programmers who are developing new applications, porting, or maintaining existing applications. If you are new to HP-UX, you will find that programming is easier with SoftBench's integrated, visual programming environment. In addition, you will find that the integrated graphical user interfaces to the system programming tools (compilers, make, sdiff, debugger), as well as the Static Analysis functionality not available in the system tools, provide a more powerful toolset than the system tools themselves.

SoftBench is a very flexible development environment. I'll cover a simple use of the SoftBench tools. You can consult the SoftBench product documentation if you need to do something more complicated.

First, let's make sure you have SoftBench installed on your system. Check for the file **/opt/softbench/bin/softbench**. If this file isn't there, then you don't have SoftBench.

Next we need to make sure that you have the SoftBench directory in your PATH. To do this type:

```
$ echo $PATH
```

The SoftBench directory needs to appear in your path before the directories **/usr/bin** and **/bin**. You should add **/opt/softbench/bin** to your environment startup file. For now, you can just modify your path in the window you will start SoftBench from as follows:

```
$ export PATH=/opt/softbench/bin:$PATH
```

Starting SoftBench

SoftBench is started by issuing the SoftBench command:

```
$ softbench
```

This will bring up the SoftBench ToolBar, as seen in Figure 12.1:

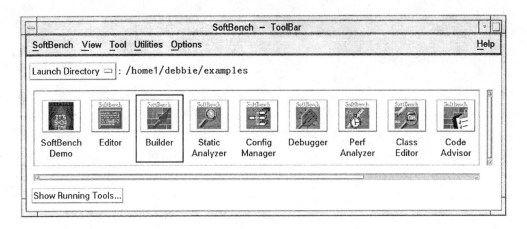

Figure 12-1 SoftBench ToolBar

The major SoftBench tools can be started from the SoftBench Tool-
Bar either by dragging an appropriate file or directory from the VUE or
CDE file managers and dropping it on a tool icon, or double-clicking a
tool icon.

Let's copy some example files to play with. Start by making a
directory for the files and then change to that directory. Let's call our
directory "examples".

```
$ mkdir examples
$ cd examples
```

Next we'll copy some files from the SoftBench directory to the
examples directory.

```
$ cp /opt/softbench/examples/Blackjack/C/* .
```

Change permissions so you have write permission:

```
$ chmod +w *
```

You should now have the following files in your directory:

```
$ ls
bj.h          bj_inst.c       bj_play.c       blackjack.c
bj_deck.c     bj_payoff.c     bj_stat.c
```

Compiling the Files

We will use the SoftBench Program Builder to compile and link the files. Start the Program Builder by double-clicking on the Builder icon in the SoftBench ToolBar. The first thing that we need to do is to create a makefile for our program. Select the *Makefile: Create/Modify Makefile...* menu button. This will bring up the dialog for specifying compiler options, include files and libraries needed to compile and link the program as shown in figure 12-2.

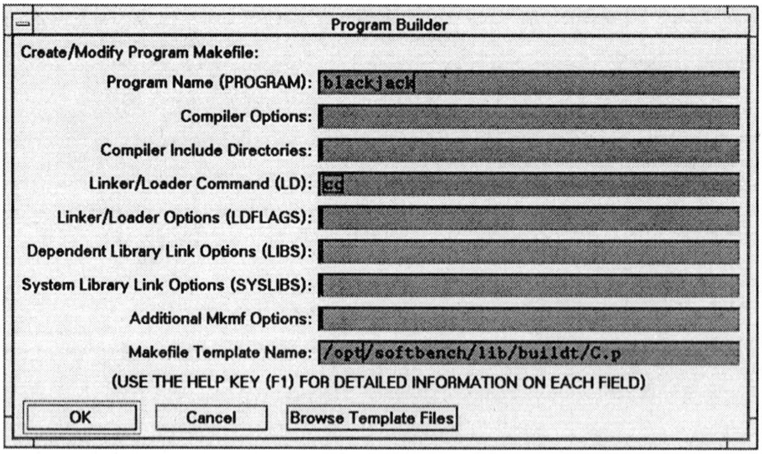

Figure 12-2   Create/Modify Program Makefile Dialog.

For this example, let's change the Program Name to **blackjack**, as shown in Figure 12-2.

This is a good time to discuss SoftBench Help. SoftBench has extensive context-sensitive on-line help. If there's something you don't understand, just press *F1* over it. For example, if you want to know what a "Linker/Loader Command (LD):" is, place the cursor over the line that says **Linker/Loader Command (LD):** in the dialog and press *F1*.

Getting back to our example, when you press **OK**, the makefile will be generated and you'll be back in the main Program Builder window.

Now we are ready to compile and link our program. Since we changed the name of our program, we need to type "**blackjack**" in the *Target: Input Area*. To begin the compile, press the *Build* button in the lower right hand corner of the Program Builder window. This will run the make utility in the current working directory with the values in the *Options* and *Target* input boxes passed to the build program. Notice that in the first line of output in the *Browser* window, *CCOPTS=-y -g*. This tells us that our code is being compiled for debugging (-g) and static analysis (-y). We'll be using these tools later.

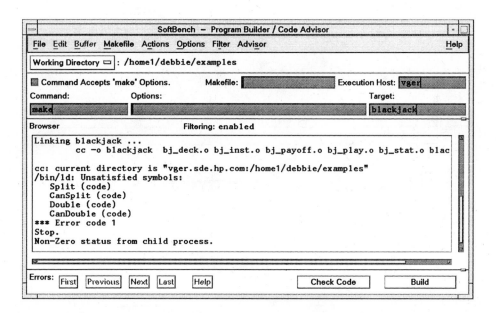

Figure 12-3   Program Builder Showing our Four Unsatisfied Symbols.

Figure 12-3 shows the results of our build. This build fails because there are four symbols (**Split**, **CanSplit**, **Double** and **CanDouble**) that are used but not defined. This gives us a chance to use the Static Analyzer and Editor to fix these problems. There are two ways to fix a problem like this, add the missing code or remove the call. We'll try both.

Starting the Static Analyzer

We'll use the SoftBench Static Analyzer to find the places where these calls are made. The Static Analyzer can be invoked from the *File: Static Analysis* menu in the Program Builder. (Of course it could also be started from the SoftBench ToolBar, but starting it from the Program Builder ensures that both tools are working on the same files.)

Like several other SoftBench tools, SoftBench Static Analyzer provides a "*( ):*" Input Box. This Input Box is used to provide input for many of the pull down menu commands. If you type "**CanDouble**" in the "*( ):*" Input Area and then select the *Show: References ( )* menu item. There will be two references to "**CanDouble**" shown in the Query window of the Static Analyzer in Figure 12-4.

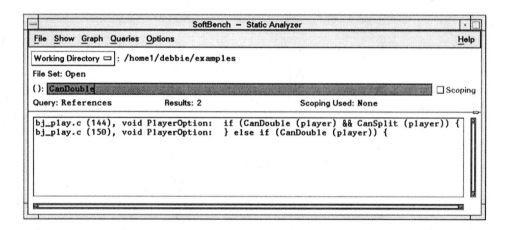

Figure 12-4   Static Analyzer Window with the Results of File: Show References on **CanDouble**

Double-click on the first entry and the Program Editor will come up on the reference to **CanDouble**. The Edit Buffer window in the Program Editor is light blue and there is a button that says "*Read-Only*" just under the *Help* menu. Press the *Read-Only* button to make the file writable. The Edit Buffer window will turn dark blue and the label on the button will change to *Save*. When you want to save changes, you press the *Save* button.

We will be removing the doubling functionality from the blackjack program, but leaving the splitting functionality. The code for the procedure PlayerOption looks like this:

```
/
****************************************************************
    PlayerOption gives the user the opportunity to Split or
Double Down his Hand, if appropriate. If not, HitPlayer() is
called for basic Hit or Stand choices.
****************************************************************/
void PlayerOption (player, deck)
    PlayerRef player;
    Deck deck;
{
    char opt = ' ';

    if (CanDouble (player) && CanSplit (player)) {
        for (opt = ' '; !strchr ("hsd/", tolower (opt)); ) {
                printf ("\nHit (h), Stand (s), Double (d),
                        or Split (/)? ");
                fflush (stdin);
                scanf ("%c", &opt);
        };
    } else if (CanDouble (player)) {
        for (opt = ' '; !strchr ("hsd", tolower (opt)); ) {
                printf ("\nHit (h), Stand (s), or Double
                        (d)? ");
                fflush (stdin);
                scanf ("%c", &opt);
        };
    } else if (CanSplit (player)) {
        for (opt = ' '; !strchr ("hs/", tolower (opt)); ) {
                printf ("\nHit (h), Stand (s), or Split (/)? ");
                fflush (stdin);
                scanf ("%c", &opt);
        };
    };

    switch (tolower (opt)) {
        case 'd':Double (player, deck);
                break;
        case '/':Split (player, deck);
                break;
```

```
        case 'h':Hit (player->hand, deck);
                printf ("\n* HIT *\n");
                show (player->hand);
               HitPlayer (player->hand, deck);
                break;
        case 's': printf ("\n* STAND *\n");
                break;
        default:HitPlayer (player->hand, deck);
                break;
    };

}
```

Let's start with the first big **if** statement at the beginning of the procedure. See how there are three cases: one for both **CanDouble** and **CanSplit**, one for just **CanDouble** and the third for just **CanSplit**? We need just the case for **CanSplit**. Comment out the other cases by making the changes shown in **bold** type:

```
/* if (CanDouble (player) && CanSplit (player)) {
    for (opt = ' '; !strchr ("hsd/", tolower (opt)); ) {
            printf ("\nHit (h), Stand (s), Double (d),
                    or Split (/)? ");
            fflush (stdin);
            scanf ("%c", &opt);
    };
} else if (CanDouble (player)) {
    for (opt = ' '; !strchr ("hsd", tolower (opt)); ) {
            printf ("\nHit (h), Stand (s), or Double
                    (d)? ");
            fflush (stdin);
            scanf ("%c", &opt);
    };
} else */ if (CanSplit (player)) {
    for (opt = ' '; !strchr ("hs/", tolower (opt)); ) {
            printf ("\nHit (h), Stand (s), or Split (/)? ");
            fflush (stdin);
            scanf ("%c", &opt);
    };
};
```

That takes care of the calls to **CanDouble**. Let's look for **Double**. If you go back to the Static Analyzer and type **Double** in the "( ):" Input Area and then *Show: References ( )*, there will be one reference. Double-click on it, and it will bring you to the first case of the switch statement in the same procedure. Comment out this case as shown in the **bold** type:

```
switch (tolower (opt)) {
    /* case 'd':Double (player, deck);
            break; */
    case '/':Split (player, deck);
            break;
    case 'h':Hit (player->hand, deck);
            printf ("\n* HIT *\n");
            show (player->hand);
            HitPlayer (player->hand, deck);
            break;
    case 's': printf ("\n* STAND *\n");
            break;
    default:HitPlayer (player->hand, deck);
            break;
};
```

Now press the *Save* button in the Program Editor, go back to the Program Builder and press the *Build* button. The build should still fail, but **CanDouble** and **Double** should be off of the list of Unsatisfied Symbols, leaving just **Split** and **CanSplit**. To satisfy these symbols, we'll add their code in a new file called **bj_split.c**. To do this, go into the Program Editor and select *File: Edit....* In the *Edit File:* dialog, replace the word **"play"** with **"split"** and hit **OK**. Add the following text in the edit buffer and press *Save*.

```
/* bj_split.c */
#include <stdio.h>
#include "bj.h"

/
*****************************************************************
    CanSplit returns True if the player's hand is eligible for
a Split:
        The two cards in his hand must be of equal rank
        The player's stake must be at least double the wager
*****************************************************************/
int CanSplit (player)
    PlayerRef player;
```

```
{
    return (((*player->hand)->rank ==
            (*player->hand)->next->rank)
            && (player->stake >= 2 * player->wager));
}


/
*************************************************************
    Split performs the actual split operation. The two cards
in the hand are separated, each is given an additional card,
then each hand is displayed and played in the normal manner.
*************************************************************/
void Split (player, deck)
    PlayerRef player;
    Deck deck;
{
    printf ("\n* SPLIT *\n");
    *player->split = (*player->hand)->next;
    (*player->hand)->next = NULL;

    Hit (player->hand, deck);
    Hit (player->split, deck);

    printf ("FIRST HAND:\n");
    show (player->hand);
    HitPlayer (player->hand, deck);

    printf ("\nSECOND HAND:\n");
    show (player->split);
    HitPlayer (player->split, deck);
}
```

If you now go back to the Program Builder and press *Build*, the Program Builder reports that "blackjack is up to date". That's because it doesn't know about the new **bj_split.c** file we just added. If you run *Makefile: Update Dependencies*, the new file will be added to the makefile. If you press the *Build* button now, the program should build successfully. If it doesn't, you can practice using the error browsing functionality in Program Builder. My favorite method is to press the *First* button and double-click on the error to bring the reported location of the error up in the Program Editor. After fixing the error, save the file and rebuild. I prefer fixing just one error at a time - or perhaps two if I know they are unrelated. Usually finding an error will confuse the compiler enough that later errors are not very accurate.

Now that the blackjack program is built, you can play with it. From the Program Builder, select *Actions: Run Target...*. The Program Builder will start a window with the prompt:

```
$ ./blackjack
```

Stretch the window as tall as you can and then hit *Return*. This will start the blackjack program. If you are not familiar with the game Black-jack, answer "**y**" to the question about whether you want instructions. The instructions are long, which is why we stretched the window. Play the game as long as you want.

There aren't any known defects in this program, but it would be good to learn to use the debugger. So we will pretend that there is a defect and make a gratuitous change to "fix" it.

Starting the Program Debugger

We'll start the Program Debugger with the *Actions: Debug Target...* menu in the Program Builder. SoftBench's Program Debugger is a window interface for HP's Distributed Debugger Environment (DDE), enhancing and extending DDE functionality, and is used to examine and control the execution of your program.

When the debugger comes up, as in Figure 12-5, it sets a breakpoint at the first executable statement, runs the program up to that statement, and then pauses. In the file buffer in the Program Debugger, there is an arrow pointing to a stop sign with the initials "BP" next to the line:

```
srand ((int) time());
```

The arrow shows the current PC (Program Counter) Location, which is the next line to be executed. The stop sign shows that there is a breakpoint set. If you scroll to the bottom of the file, you'll notice that the debugger has set a breakpoint at the end of the program. This gives you one last chance to restart the debugger on the program without having to reload all of the debug information.

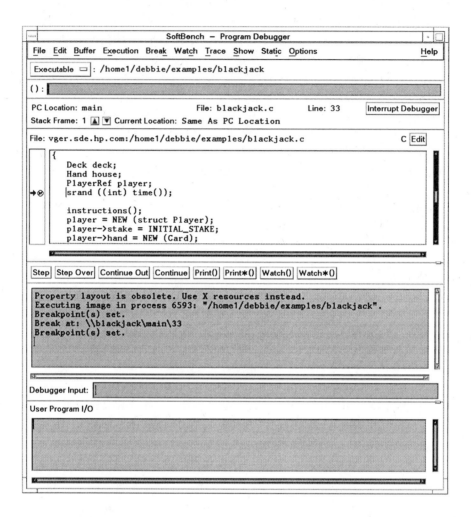

Figure 12-5   Debugger Window

Let's play with the stepping and breakpoint commands before we go looking for code to change. There are four step and continue user buttons in the default configuration: *Step*, *Step Over*, *Continue Out* and *Continue*.

Press *Step*. The srand line will be executed and the arrow advances to the line with the call to instructions(). Press *Step* again. This time we step into the instructions() procedure. Why did we skip over the call to time() and step into the instructions procedure?

Press *Continue Out*. Several changes happened on the Program Debugger window: the line for PC Location has an animated clock and inverse video line that says "Running..." and down in the User Program I/O buffer at the bottom of the window it says

```
Casino BlackJack

Do you want instructions?
```

The blackjack program is waiting to hear whether you want instructions. If the program had gone into an infinite loop or was having some other trouble, it is likely that the Program Debugger would look like this, but without the text in the User Program I/O buffer. In that case, the *Interrupt Program* button would send a signal to stop the program so the debugger could regain control. Fortunately our program doesn't have a major problem - it just wants some input. Since you've already read the instructions, move the mouse pointer over the User Program I/O buffer and type "*n*" and then hit *Return*.

Now the debugger is back in control and we have returned from the call to the instructions procedure. Let's try setting a breakpoint. If you move the mouse pointer to the buffer to the left of the source buffer (where the arrow and breakpoint symbols are), you can see that the cursor has changed into a breakpoint symbol. If you single-click, a breakpoint will be set at that location. Set a breakpoint at the line that says:

```
player->split = NEW (Card);
```

With the breakpoint set, we can have the debugger execute all of the instructions between our current location and the breakpoint by pressing the *Continue* user menu button. Notice that the arrow is now on the same line as the breakpoint you just set. This shows that the program has executed up to the breakpoint location and paused. Now scroll down a little and set a breakpoint at the line:

```
PlaceBet (player);
```

Press *Continue* to have the program execute to the breakpoint. (You will need to type "*p*" and *Return* in the User Program I/O area so the cards can be shuffled.) Double-click on the word "player" in the Place-Bet call. This copies the word "player" to the "*( )*:" Input Box. Press the *Print()* user button. The value of player is displayed in the debugger output area, just below the user buttons. Since player is a pointer, a large hex number is displayed. Now press the *Print*()* user button. This follows the pointer and prints the player record.

Remember that gratuitous change we were going to make? Let's pretend that we want our blackjack game based on 25 points in a hand, instead of 21. We could step through the program until we see where a test is made against the number 21, or we could take a wild guess that it is in the procedure called TwentyOne. *Step* into the TwentyOne procedure. Since this is a small change, we can make it right in the debugger. Press the *Edit* button just above the source buffer. The source buffer changes to dark blue, indicating that the buffer is writable. Change 21 to 25 and press the *Save* button. To get the change to take effect, we need to recompile the program. The easy way to do this is with the *File: Fix Executable* menu button. Try this and notice the flurry of activity. The blackjack program is unloaded from the debugger, the Program Builder recompiles and links blackjack, and blackjack is reloaded into the Program Debugger with the program paused at the first breakpoint. If you scroll down a little, you can see that your breakpoints have even been restored.

Figure 12-6 summarizes the four commands we have been working with.

Step	Execute one statement, then stop, This is called **single step** execution.
Step Over	Execute a statement, treating any procedure call as a single statement. The procedure is called, but control does not return to the debugger until the procedure returns. When the PC is just before a procedure call, this has the effect of "stepping over" the call.

Continue Out	Finish executing the current procedure. Run without stepping until the current procedure completes and returns to its caller (or until another breakpoint or similar event is encountered), then stop. This is very useful when you accidentally step into a procedure that you do not want to step through, or when you interrupt your program in the middle of nondebuggable code. Each **Continue Out** will cause your program to "pop out" one procedure level.
Continue	Execute the program until the next breakpoint is hit. If there are no more breakpoints, the program will finish.

Figure 12-6 *Step* and *Continue* User Menu Commands

If you play the modified program awhile, you will notice that there are a couple things wrong. First, the algorithm for calculating the score when you have one or more aces is a little off, and second, it still reports that you went bust when your score is between 21 and 24. See if you can find and fix these two remaining errors.

More About SoftBench

This chapter provided a small hint of the capability of SoftBench. There are several more tools available, including two other editors, a performance analyzer, a file comparison tool and a file manager. In addition, there is a lot of functionality that we didn't cover in the Program Builder, Program Debugger, and Static Analyzer. You can find out about these features in the manual (there is an electronic version of all the manuals on the SoftBench CD if you don't have printed manuals), and in the on-line Tutorial, which is available from the SoftBench ToolBar.

If you would like to contact the SoftBench team, you can use the Customer Services tool available from the SoftBench ToolBar, or check out our Web page at **http://www.hp.com/go/softbench**.

Chapter 13

Command Summary

Command Summaries

This chapter consists of summaries of the commands from all the previous chapters. These are *abbreviated* command summaries. I include only the most commonly used options to commands and provide an example of how most commands can be used. For complete descriptions of commands you should refer to the manual pages for commands.

Since this book is an introduction to HP-UX, it contains the most commonly used HP-UX commands. This is by no means an exhaustive list of commands. If, however, you can use the commands covered in this book you are well on your way to mastering HP-UX.

cat

cat - Display, combine, append, copy, or create files.

Options

-	Used as a substitute for specifying a file name when you want to use the keyboard for standard input.
-n	Line numbers are displayed along with output lines.
-p	Replace multiple consecutive empty lines with only one empty line.
-s	This is silent mode which suppresses information about nonexistent files.
-u	Output is unbuffered, which means it is handled character by character.
-v	Print most nonprinting characters visibly.

```
                              cat −n example
   106   rclock.exe
   107   rkhelp.exe
   108   sb.txt
   109   shellupd.exe
   110   smsup2.exe
   111   softinit.remotesoftcm
   112   srvpr.exe
   113   tabnd1.exe
   114   target.exe
   115   tcp41a.exe
   116   tnds2.exe
   117   trace.TRC1
   118   trace.TRC1.Z.uue
   119   upgrade.exe
   120   uue.syntax
   121   v103.txt
   122   whoon
   123   win95app.exe
   124   wsdrv1.exe
   125   wsos21.exe
   126   wsos22.exe
   127   wsos23.exe
   128   xferp110.zip
$
```

cd

cd - Change to a new current directory

Arguments

none	Change to home directory. This is defined by the HOME environment variable
..	The two dot notation moves you to the parent directory of your current directory.
path	You can specify either an absolute or relative path to change to.

```
$ pwd
/tmp
$ cd $HOME
$ pwd
/home/denise
$
```

chmod

chmod - Change permissions of specified files using the following symbolic mode list.

Symbol of who is affected:

u	User is affected.
g	Group is affected.
o	Other is affected.
a	All users are affected.

Operation to perform:

+	Add permission.
-	Remove permission.
=	Replace permission.

Permission specified:

r	Read permission.
w	Write permission.
x	Execute permission.
u	Copy user permissions.
g	Copy group permissions.
o	Copy other permissions.

Numeric Mode Example:

```
$ ls -l sort
-rwxr-x--x   1 marty      users      120 Jul 26 10:20 sort

$ chmod 770 sort
```

```
$ ls -l sort
-rwxrwx---   1 marty       users      120 Jul 26 10:20 sort
```

Symbolic Mode Example:

```
$ ls -l sort
-rwxr-x--x   1 marty       users      120 Jul 26 10:20 sort

$ chmod g+w,o-x sort

$ ls -l sort
-rwxrwx---   1 marty       users      120 Jul 26 10:20 sort
```

cmp

cmp - Compare the contents of two files. The byte position and line number of the first difference between the two files is returned.

Options

      -l   Display the byte position and differing characters for all differences within a file.

      -s   Work silently, that is only exit codes are returned.

```
$
$ cmp llsum llsum.orig
llsum llsum.orig differ: char 154, line 6
$
```

```
$ cmp -l llsum llsum.orig
     154   62   61
     155   65   66
     306   62   61
     307   65   66
     675   62   61
     676   65   66
```

cp

cp - Copy files and directories.

Options

-i	Interactive copy whereby you are prompted to confirm you wish to overwrite an existing file.
-f	Force existing files to be overwritten by files being copied if there is a conflict in file names.
-p	Preserve permissions when copying.
-r	Copy recursively.
-R	Copy recursively except permissions are different.

```
$ mkdir ../krsort.dir.new
$ cp krsort ../krsort.dir.new
$ ls -l ../krsort.dir.new
total 68
-rwxr-xr-x   1 denise   users      34592 Oct 27 18:27 krsort
$
```

cut

cut - Extract specified fields from each line.

Options

    -c list   Extract based on character position as shown in the example.

    -f list   Extract based on fields.

    -d char The character following d is the delimiter when using the -f option. The delimiter is the character which separates fields.

```
$ llsum | cut -c 1-25,37-43

FILENAME                      SIZE
README                         810
backup_files                  3408
biography                      427
cshtest                       1024
gkill                         1855
gkill.out                      191
hostck                         924
ifstat                        1422
ifstat.int                    2147
ifstat.out                     723
introdos                     54018
introux                      52476
letter                       23552
letter.auto                  69632
letter.auto.recover          71680
letter.backup                23552
letter.lck                      57
letter.recover               69632
llsum                         1267
llsum.orig                    1267
llsum.out                     1657
llsum.tomd.out                1356
psg                            670
psg.int                        802
psg.out                        122
sam_adduser                   1010
tdolan                        1024
trash                         4554
trash.out                      329
typescript                      74

The files listed occupy 3 (0.373
Average file size is 1305
$
```

diff

diff - Compare two files and report differing lines.

___

Options

-b	Ignore blanks at the end of a line.
-i	Ignore case differences.
-t	Expand tabs in output to spaces.
-w	Ignore spaces and tabs.

```
$ diff llsum llsum.orig
6c6
< awk ' BEGIN { x=i=0; printf "%-25s%-10s%8s%8s\n",\
---
> awk ' BEGIN { x=i=0; printf "%-16s%-10s%8s%8s\n",\
9c9
<               printf "%-25s%-10s%8d",$9,$3,$5
---
>               printf "%-16s%-10s%8d",$9,$3,$5
19c19
<               printf "%-25s%-10s%8s%8s\n",$10,$3,"","dev"
---
>               printf "%-16s%-10s%8s%8s\n",$10,$3,"","dev"
$
```

dircmp

dircmp - Compare directories.

Options

-d   Compare the contents of files with the same name in both directories and produce a report of what must be done to make the files identical.

-s   Suppress information about different files.

```
$ dircmp krsort.dir.old krsort.dir.new


krsort.dir.old only and krsort.dir.new only Page 1


./krsort.c          ./krsort.test.c




Comparison of krsort.dir.old krsort.dir.new Page 1


directory        .
same          ./krsort
same          ./krsort.dos
same          ./krsort.q
same          ./krsortorig.c

$
```

ftp

ftp - File Transfer Program for copying files across a network.

The following list includes some commonly used **ftp** commands. This list is not complete.

ascii   User is affected. Set the type of file transferred to ASCII. This means you will be transferring an ASCII file from one system to another. This is the default so you don't have to set it.

      Example: **ascii**

binary   Set the type of file transferred to binary. This means you'll be transferring a binary file from one system to another. If, for instance, you want to have a directory on your HP-UX system which will hold applications that you will copy to non-HP-UX systems, then you will want to use binary transfer.

      Example: **binary**

cd   Change to the specified directory on the remote host.

      Example: **cd /tmp**

dir   List the contents of a directory on the remote system to the screen or to a file on the local system if you specify a local file name.

get   Copy the specified remote file to the specified local file. If you don't specify a local file name, then the remote file name will be used.

lcd   Change to the specified directory on the local host.

Example: **lcd /tmp**

ls   List the contents of a directory on the remote system to the screen or to a file on the local system if you specify a local file name.

mget   Copy multiple files from the remote host to the local host.

Example: **mget *.c**

put   Copy the specified local file to the specified remote file. If you don't specify a remote file name, then the local file name will be used.

Example: **put test.c**

mput   Copy multiple files from the local host to the remote host.

Example: **mput *.c**

system   Show the type of operating system running on the remote host.

Example: **system**

bye/quit   Close the connection to the remote host.

Example: **bye**

	comments
$ ftp system2	Issue ftp command
Connected to system2.	
system2 FTP server (Version 16.2) ready.	
Name (system2:root): root	Login to system2
Password required for root.	
Password:	Enter password
User root logged in.	
Remote system type is UNIX.	
Using binary mode to transfer files.	
ftp> **cd /tmp**	**cd** to **/tmp** on system2
CWD command successful	
ftp> **get krsort.c**	Get **krsort.c** file
PORT command successful	
Opening BINARY mode data connection for **krsort.c**	
Transfer complete.	
2896 bytes received in 0.08 seconds	
ftp> **bye**	Exit ftp
Goodbye.	
$	

grep

grep - Search for text and displays result.

Options

-c	Return the number of matches without showing you the text.
-h	Show the text with no reference to file names.
-i	Ignore the case when searching.
-l	Return the names of files containing a match without showing you the text.
-n	Return the line number of the text searched for in a file as well as the text itself.
-v	Return the lines that do not match the text you searched for.
-E	Search for more than one expression (same as **egrep**).
-F	Search for more than one expression (same as **fgrep**).

```
                              grep example
$ ls -a /home/denise | grep netscape
.netscape-bookmarks.html
.netscape-cache
.netscape-history
.netscape-newsgroups-news.spry.com
.netscape-newsgroups-newsserv.hp.com
.netscape-preferences
$ ls -a /home/denise | grep -c netscape
6
$ ls -a /home/denise | grep NETSCAPE
$ ls -a /home/denise | grep -i NETSCAPE
.netscape-bookmarks.html
.netscape-cache
.netscape-history
.netscape-newsgroups-news.spry.com
.netscape-newsgroups-newsserv.hp.com
.netscape-preferences
$ ls -a /home/denise | grep -F "netscape
> .c"
.cshrc
.cshrc.orig
.netscape-bookmarks.html
.netscape-cache
.netscape-history
.netscape-newsgroups-news.spry.com
.netscape-newsgroups-newsserv.hp.com
.netscape-preferences
.newsrc-news.spry.com
.newsrc-newsserv.hp.com
$ ▊
```

head

head - Provide only the first few lines of a file.

Options

-c	The output is produced with a specified number of bytes.
-l	The output is produced with a specified number of lines. This is the default.
-n count	The number of bytes or lines is specified by count. You can also use -count to specify the number of bytes or lines which is shown in the example. The default count is 10.

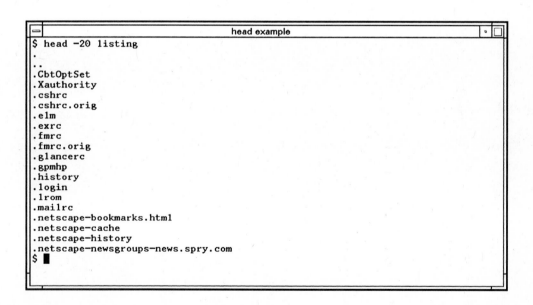

```
                              head example
$ head -20 listing
.
..
.CbtOptSet
.Xauthority
.cshrc
.cshrc.orig
.elm
.exrc
.fmrc
.fmrc.orig
.glancerc
.gpmhp
.history
.login
.lrom
.mailrc
.netscape-bookmarks.html
.netscape-cache
.netscape-history
.netscape-newsgroups-news.spry.com
$ █
```

join

join - Combine two presorted files that have a common key field.

Options

        -a n   Produce the normal output and also generate a line for each line that can't be joined in 1 or 2.

        -e string Replace empty fields in output with string.

        -t char Use char as the field separator.

ls

ls - List the contents of a directory

Options

-a	List all entries.
-b	Print nongraphic characters.
-c	Use time file was last modified for producing order in which files are listed.
-d	List only the directory name, not its contents.
-f	Assume each argument is a directory.
-g	Only the group is printed and not the owner.
-i	Print the inode number in the first column of the report.
-m	List the contents across the screen separated by commas.
-n	Numbers for UID and GID are printed instead of names.
-o	List the information in long form (-l) except that group is omitted.
-p	Put a slash (/) at the end of directory names.
-q	Nonprinting characters are represented by a "?".
-r	Reverse the order in which files are printed.
-s	Show the size in blocks instead of bytes.
-t	List in order of time saved with most recent first.
-u	Use time of last access instead of last modification for determining order in which files are printed.
-x	List files in multicolumn format as shown in examples.
-A	Same as -a except current and parent directories aren't listed.
-C	Multicolumn output produced.
-F	Directory followed by a "/", executable by an "*", symbolic link by an "@", and FIFO by a "|".
-L	List file or directory to which link points.
-R	Recursively list subdirectories.
-1	Output will be listed in single column format.

```
$ ls -p /home/denise

.Xauthority
.cshrc
.elm/
.exrc
.fmrc.orig
.glancerc
.gpmhp
.history
.login
.lrom/
.mailrc
.netscape-bookmarks.html
.netscape-cache/
.netscape-cookies
.netscape-history
.netscape-newsgroups-news.spry.com
.netscape-newsgroups-newsserv.hp.com
.netscape-preferences
.newsrc-news.spry.com
.newsrc-newsserv.hp.com
.profile
.rhosts
.sh_history
.softbuildrc
.softinit.orig
.sw/
.vue/
.vueprofile
.xinitrc
.xsession
27247b.exe
410pt1.exe
410pt2.exe
41ndir.exe
41nds1.exe
41nds4.exe
41nwad.exe
41rtr2.exe
HPDA1.EXE
Mail/
N3212B6.EXE
SCSI4S.EXE
clean
clean2
clean3
content.exe
dsenh.exe
eg1
eg2
en0316bz.exe
en0316tb.exe
explore.exe
flexi_cd.exe
fred.h
hal.c
hpdl0117.exe
hpdlinst.txt
hpux.patches
j2577a.exe
ja95up.exe
msie10.exe
n32e12n.exe
nfs197.exe
pass.sb
plusdemo.exe
ps4x03.exe
psg
quik_res.exe
rclock.exe
rkhelp.exe
roni.mak
sb.txt
smsup2.exe
```

```
softinit.remotesoftcm
srvpr.exe
steve.h
target.exe
tcp41a.exe
tnds2.exe
upgrade.exe
whoon
win95app.exe
```

mkdir

mkdir - Create specified directories.

Options

-m   Specify the mode (permissions) of the directory.

-p   Create intermediate directories to achieve the full path. If
        you want to create several layers of directory down you
        would use **-p**.

```
$ mkdir -p level1/level2/level3
$ ls -R level1
level2

level1/level2:
level3

level1/level2/level3:
$
```

more

more - Display all or parts of a file on screen at a time.

Options

-c   Clear the screen before displaying the next page of the file.

-d   Display a prompt at the bottom of the screen with brief instructions.

-f   Wrap text to fit screen and judges page length accordingly.

-n   The number of lines in the display window is set to n.

-s   Squeeze multiple consecutive empty lines into one empty line.

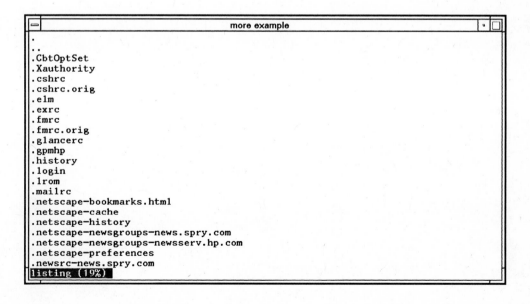

mv

mv - Copy files and directories.

___

Options

-i	Interactive copy whereby you are prompted to confirm you wish to over write an existing file.
-f	Force existing files to be overwritten by files being copied if there is a conflict in file names.
-p	Preserve permissions when copying.

```
$ mv krsort.c krsort.test.c
$ ls -l
total 168
-rwxr-xr-x    1 denise    users        34592 Oct 31 15:17 krsort
-rwxr-xr-x    1 denise    users        32756 Oct 31 15:17 krsort.dos
-rw-r--r--    1 denise    users         9922 Oct 31 15:17 krsort.q
-rwxr-xr-x    1 denise    users         3234 Oct 31 15:17 krsort.test.c
-rwxr-xr-x    1 denise    users         3085 Oct 31 15:17 krsortorig.c
$
```

paste

paste - Merge lines of files.

Options

-d list   Use list as the delimiter between columns. You can use special escape sequences for list such as \n for newline and \t for tab.

```
$ paste llsum.out ll.out

FILENAME                    SIZE        total 792
README                       810        -rwxrwxrwx
backup_files                3408        -rwxrwxrwx
biography                    427        -rwxrwxrwx
cshtest                     1024        drwxr-xr-x
gkill                       1855        -rwxrwxrwx
gkill.out                    191        -rw-r--r--
hostck                       924        -rwxrwxrwx
ifstat                      1422        -rwxrwxrwx
ifstat.int                  2147        -rwxr-xr-x
ifstat.out                   723        -rw-r--r--
introdos                   54018        -rw-r--r--
introux                    52476        -rwxrwxrwx
letter                     23552        -rw-r--r--
letter.auto                69632        -rw-r--r--
letter.auto.recover        71680        -rw-r--r--
letter.backup              23552        -rw-r--r--
letter.lck                    57        -rw-rw-rw-
letter.recover             69632        -rw-r--r--
ll.out                      1057        -rw-r--r--
llsum                       1267        -rwxrwxrwx
llsum.orig                  1267        -rwxr-xr-x
llsum.out                   1657        -rw-r--r--
llsum.tomd.out              1356        -rw-r--r--
psg                          670        -rwxrwxrwx
psg.int                      802        -rwxr-xr-x
psg.out                      122        -rw-r--r--
sam_adduser                 1010        -rwxrwxrwx
tdolan                      1024        drwxr-xr-x
trash                       4554        -rwxrwxrwx
trash.out                    329        -rw-r--r--
typescript                   679        -rw-r--r--

$
```

pg

pg - Display all or parts of a file.

Options

-number   The number of lines you wish to display.

-p string Use string to specify a prompt.

-c   Clear the screen before displaying the next page of the file.

-f   Don't split lines being displayed.

-n   A command is issued as soon as a command letter is typed rather than having to issue a new line character.

```
pg example
.
..
.CbtOptSet
.Xauthority
.cshrc
.cshrc.orig
.elm
.exrc
.fmrc
.fmrc.orig
.glancerc
.gpmhp
.history
.login
.lrom
.mailrc
.netscape-bookmarks.html
.netscape-cache
.netscape-history
.netscape-newsgroups-news.spry.com
.netscape-newsgroups-newsserv.hp.com
.netscape-preferences
.newsrc-news.spry.com
:
```

pwd

pwd - Print Working Directory so you know your current location.

Examples

```
$ pwd
/home/denise/.netscape-cache
$ cd ..
$ pwd
/home/denise
$
```

rcp

rcp - Remote file copy.

Options and Arguments:

              source file   This <u>argument</u> is the name of a file you wish to copy to a remote system or from a remote system.

       source directory   This <u>argument</u> is the name of a directory you wish to copy to a remote system or from a remote system.

      destination file   This <u>argument</u> is the file name to which a file will be copied.

destination directory   This <u>argument</u> is the directory name to which a directory will be copied.

             -p   This <u>option</u> preserves information about the source files. Such information as permissions and modification times are preserved for files copied.

             -r   This <u>option</u> performs a recursive copy. You can copy subdirectories of the source directory name using this option.

```
$ rcp    system2:/tmp/krsort.c  /tmp/krsort.c
```

Redirection

Command	Example	Description
I	**ll I grep .login**	Perform a long listing and search for the text **.login**
<	**wc -l < .login**	Standard input redirection: execute **wc** (word count) and list number of lines (**-l**) in **.login**
>	**ps -ef > /tmp/processes**	Standard output redirection: execute **ps** and send output to file **/tmp/processes**
>>	**ps -ef >> /tmp/processes**	Append standard output: execute **ps** and append output to the end of file **/tmp/processes**
>!	**ps -ef >! /tmp/processes**	Append output redirection and override **noclobber**: write over **/tmp/processes** even if it exists
>>!	**ps -ef >>! /tmp/processes**	Append standard output and override **noclobber**: append to the end of **/tmp/processes**

remsh

remsh - Execute a command on a remote system.

Options and Arguments:

remote host   This <u>argument</u> is the name of the remote host on which
               you wish to run the command.

-l user name   This <u>option</u> allows you to specify the name of a user you
               wish to run the command as on the remote system.

```
$ remsh system2 ll /tmp/krsort.c
-rwxrwxrwx 1 root sys 2896 Sept 1 10:54 /tmp/krsort.c
$
```

rlogin

rlogin - Remote login.

Options and Arguments:

remote host   This <u>argument</u> is the name of the remote host you wish to log in to.

-l user name   This <u>option</u> allows you to specify the name of a user you wish to log in on the remote system.

```
$ rlogin system2
password:
Welcome to system2
$
```

rm

rm - Remove files and directories.

Options

-i   Interactive remove whereby you are prompted to confirm
          you wish to remove an existing file.

-f   Force files to be removed.

-r (-R)   Recursively remove the contents of the directory and
          then the directory itself.

```
$ rm -i ../krsort.dir.new/*
../krsort.dir.new/krsort: ? (y/n) y
../krsort.dir.new/krsort.c: ? (y/n) y
../krsort.dir.new/krsort.dos: ? (y/n) y
../krsort.dir.new/krsort.q: ? (y/n) y
../krsort.dir.new/krsortorig.c: ? (y/n) y
$ ls -al ../krsort.dir.new
total 4
drwxr-xr-x   2 denise    users          1024 Oct 27 18:57 .
drwxrwxr-x   4 denise    users          1024 Oct 27 18:40 ..
-rw-r--r--   1 denise    users             0 Oct 27 18:56 .dotfile
```

rmdir

rmdir - Remove directories.

Options

-i   Interactive remove whereby you are prompted to confirm you wish to remove a directory

-f   Force directories to be removed.

-p   If, after removing a directory, the parent directory is empty then remove it also. This goes on until a parent directory is encountered that is not empty.

```
$ ls -al ../krsort.dir.new
total 4
drwxr-xr-x    2 denise    users         1024 Oct 27 18:57 .
drwxrwxr-x    4 denise    users         1024 Oct 27 18:40 ..
-rw-r--r--    1 denise    users            0 Oct 27 18:56 .dotfile
$ rmdir -i ../krsort.dir.new
../krsort.dir.new: ? (y/n) y
rmdir: ../krsort.dir.new: Directory not empty
$ rm ../krsort.dir.new/.dotfile
$ rmdir -i ../krsort.dir.new
../krsort.dir.new: ? (y/n) y
$
```

rwho

rwho - Show users logged in on remote systems.

Options and Arguments:

          -l   This <u>option</u> will include in the output list users who have not typed any information in an hour or more. These users would otherwise be omitted.

```
$ rwho
root        system1:ttyu0    Sept 1 19:21
root        system2:console  Sept 1 13:17
tomd        system2:ttyp2    Sept 1 13:05
  |             |       |          |        |-> time of login
  |             |       |          |-> day of login
  |             |       |
  |             |       |-> terminal line
  |             |-> machine name
  |
  |-> user name
```

sort

sort - Sort lines of files (alphabetically by default).

Options

-b	Ignore leading spaces and tabs.
-c	Check if files are already sorted and if so do nothing.
-d	Ignore punctuation and sort in dictionary order
-f	Ignore the case of entries when sorting.
-i	Ignore non-ASCII characters when sorting.
-m	Merge sorted files.
-n	Sort in numeric order.
-o file	Specify the output file name rather than write to standard output.
-r	Reverse order of the sort by starting with the last letter of the alphabet or with the largest number as we did in the example.
+n	Skip n fields or columns before sorting.

```
                              sort example #2
$ sort -n -r disk_space -o disk_space_numeric
$
$ head -20 disk_space_numeric
288238  main.directory
60336   emacs-19.28.tar
8128    c3295n_a.exe
5024    trace.TRC1
4496    rkhelp.exe
3840    tnds2.exe
3520    n32e12n.exe
3520    N3212B6.EXE
3056    41nwad.exe
2784    nsh220e2.zip
2768    nsh220e3.zip
2752    nfs197.exe
2688    mbox
2160    msie10.exe
2032    nsh220e1.zip
2000    trace.TRC1.Z.uue
1984    plusdemo.exe
1840    ja95up.exe
1776    hpd10117.exe
1712    wsos22.exe
$ █
```

split

split - Split a file into multiple files.

Options

-l line_count	Split the file into files with line_count lines per file.
-b n	Split the file into files with n bytes per file.

```
                               split example
$ ll listing
-rw--------   1 denise    users         1430 Dec 19 16:30 listing
$
$ split -l 25 listing
$
$ ll x*
-rw--------   1 denise    users          330 Dec 19 16:40 xaa
-rw--------   1 denise    users          267 Dec 19 16:40 xab
-rw--------   1 denise    users          268 Dec 19 16:40 xac
-rw--------   1 denise    users          256 Dec 19 16:40 xad
-rw--------   1 denise    users          274 Dec 19 16:40 xae
-rw--------   1 denise    users           35 Dec 19 16:40 xaf
$ ▮
```

tail

tail - Provide the last few lines of a file.

Options

-bnumber Specify number of blocks from end of file you wish to begin displaying.

-cnumber Specify number of characters from end of file you wish to begin displaying.

-nnumber Specify number of lines from end of file you wish to begin displaying. You can also specify a number or minus sign and number as shown in the example to specify the number of lines from the end of file to begin displaying.

```
tail example
$ tail -20 listing
shellupd.exe
smsup2.exe
softinit.remotesoftcm
srvpr.exe
tabnd1.exe
target.exe
tcp41a.exe
tnds2.exe
trace.TRC1
trace.TRC1.Z.uue
upgrade.exe
uue.syntax
v103.txt
whoon
win95app.exe
wsdrv1.exe
wsos21.exe
wsos22.exe
wsos23.exe
xferp110.zip
$
```

telnet

telnet - Communicate with another system using TELNET protocol.

The following list includes some commonly used **telnet** commands. This list is by no means complete.

open host Open a connection to the specified host. I like to use the term system in place of host, but host is the official terminology. The system you specify can be either an official name or an alias you use to connect to the system.

close   After completing your **telnet** work you should terminate your connection with this command.

quit   This command closes any open TELNET sessions and exits you from **telnet**.

?   If you type only a "?" you get a help summary. If you type a "?" and a command name then you get help information about that command.

	comments
$ telnet system2	
Connected to system2.	Telnet to system2
HP-UX system2	
login: **root**	Log in as root on system2
password:	Enter password
Welcome to system2.	
$	HP-UX prompt on system2

tr

tr - Translate characters.

Options

-A   Translate on a byte by byte basis.

-d   Delete all occurrences of characters specified.

[:class:] Translate from one character class to another such as
          from lower case class to upper case class as shown in the
          example.

```
$ ls -al *.zip
file1.zip
file2.zip
file3.zip
file4.zip
file5.zip
file6.zip
file7.zip
$ ls -al *.zip | tr "[:lower:]" "[:upper:]"
FILE1.ZIP
FILE2.ZIP
FILE3.ZIP
FILE4.ZIP
FILE5.ZIP
FILE6.ZIP
FILE7.ZIP
$
```

vi

vi - Launch the **vi** text editor.

The following tables summarize some of the more commonly used functionality of the **vi** editor.

Starting a vi Session

vi file	Edit **file.**
vi -r file	Edit last saved version of **file** after a crash.
vi -R file	Edit the file in read only mode.
vi + file	Edit **file** and place cursor on last line.
vi file1 file2 file3 ...	Edit **file1** through **file3** and after saving changes in **file1** you can move to **file2** by entering **:n**.

Cursor Control Commands in vi

Command	Cursor Movement
h	Move left one character.
j	Move down one line.
k	Move up one line.
l or space	Move right one character.
G	Go to the end of the file.
nG	Go to line number n.
G$	Go to the last character in the file.
w	Go to the beginning of the next word.
b	Go to the beginning of the previous word.
L	Go to the last line of the screen.
M	Go to the middle line of the screen.
H	Go to the first line of the screen.
e	Move to the end of the next word.
(	Go to the beginning of the sentence.
)	Go to the end of the sentence.
{	Go to the beginning of the paragraph.
}	Go to the beginning of the next paragraph.

Adding Text in vi

Command	Insertion Action
a	Append new text after the cursor.
i	Insert new text before the cursor.
o	Open a line below the current line.
O	Open a line above the current line.
:r file	Read file and insert after current line.
escape	Get back to command mode.

Deleting Text in vi

Command	Deletion Action
x	Delete the character at the cursor. You can also put a number in front of x to specify the number of characters to delete.
X	Delete the previous character. You can also put a number in front of X to specify the number of previous characters to delete.
dw	Delete to the beginning of the next word.
dG	Delete lines to the end of the file.
dd	Delete the entire line.

Command	Deletion Action
db	Delete the previous word. You can also put a number in front of db to specify the number of previous words to delete.

Changing Text in vi

Command (Preceding these commands with a number repeats the commands any number of times.)	Replacement Action
rX	Replace the current character with **X**.
R	Replace the current characters until *escape* is entered.
cw	Change to the beginning of the next word.
cG	Change to the end of the file.
cc	Change the entire line.

Search and Replace in vi

Command	Search and Replace Action
/text	Search for **text** going forward into the file.
?text	Search for **text** going backward into the file.
n	Repeat search in the same direction as the original search.
N	Repeat the search in the opposite direction as the original search.
:s/oldtext/newtext/	Substitute **newtext** for **oldtext**.
:m,ns/oldtext/newtext/	Substitute **newtext** for **oldtext** in lines **m** through **n**.

Copying in vi

Command	Copy Action
yy	Yank the current line.
nyy	Yank **n** lines.
p (lower case)	Put yanked text after cursor.
p (upper case)	Put yanked text before cursor.

Undo in vi

Command	Undo Action
u	Undo the last change.
U	Undo all changes to the current line.
. (period)	Repeat the last change.

Saving Text and Exiting vi

Command	Save and/or Quit Action
:w	Save the file but don't exit **vi**.
:w filename	Save changes in the file **filename** but don't quit **vi**.
:wq	Save the file and quit **vi**.
:q!	Quit **vi** without saving the file.

vi Options

Option	Action
:set all	Print all options.
:set no*option*	Turn off *option*.
:set nu	Prefix lines with line number.

Option	Action
:set ro	Set file to read only.
:set showmode	Show whether input or replace mode.
:set warn	Print a warning message if there has not been a write since the last change to the file.

WC

wc - Produce a count of words, lines, and characters.

Options

-l	Print the number of lines in a file.
-w	Print the number of words in a file.
-c	Print the number of characters in a file.

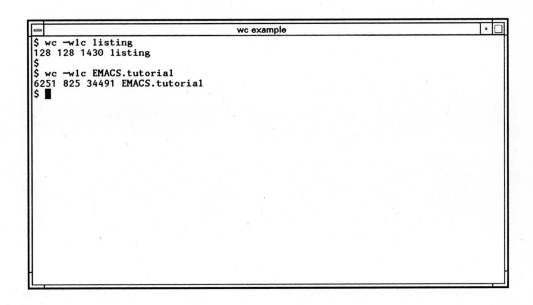

```
                                wc example
$ wc —wlc listing
128 128 1430 listing
$
$ wc —wlc EMACS.tutorial
6251 825 34491 EMACS.tutorial
$ █
```

INDEX

executable files, 30, 33-34, 37
execute permission, 52-53

F

fsck, 43
file command, 36
file manager (HP VUE), 8, 196-197
file name expansion, 71-73
file system layout, 39-48
floppy, 1
front panel (HP VUE), 190-191
  adding to, 202-205
ftp, 143-146
  ftp summary, 144-146, 272-275

G

grep, 116-117
  grep summary, 117, 276
group access, 51
group ID, 18-19

H

/home, 43, 54
head, 109-110
  head summary, 112, 277
HFS, 39
highly centralized, 10
highly distributed, 4
home directory, 19
HP 500, 9
HP 9000
  Series, 700, 40
  Series 800, 40
HP Task Broker, 5, 6
HP CDE, 2, 10, 22, 188
HP SoftBench, 247-262
  compiling files, 250-252
  more about, 261
  program debugger, 257-261
  starting, 248-250
  static analyzer, 252-257
HP VUE, 2, 6, 7, 10, 22, 188-206

HP VUE menu, 200-202
HP Wabi, 31

I

icon manager, 9
Insignia SoftWindows, 31
IP addressing, 139-142
ISO/OSI model, 135-136

J

join, 132
  command summary, 278

K

keyboard, 29
Korn shell, 154, 155

L

/lost+found, 43
load balance, 5
LaserROM, 28, 30
last command, 25, 26
lasb command, 25
link layer, 137-138
links, 30, 35
LOFS, 40
login, 15-28
login manager, 8
looping (shell prog), 173-175
ls, 49, 56-71, 92, 94, 95, 97, 98, 100, 101, 102
  ls -a, 57-59
  ls -i, 62-63
  ls -l, 59-62
  ls -p, 63-65
  ls -R, 65-69
  ls summary, 69-71, 279-281

X